D0423320

MORE SERMONS
FROM THE
MYSTERY BOX

MORE SERMONS FROM THE MYSTERY BOX

Object Lessons for Children

R. Douglas Reinard

Abingdon Press

MORE SERMONS FROM THE MYSTERY BOX:
Object Lessons for Children

This book is printed on acid-free, recycled paper.

ISBN 0-687-27186-X

Scripture quotations are taken from The Holy Bible: New International Version. Copyright © 1973, 1978, 1984 by the International Bible Society. Used by permission of Zondervan Bible Publishers.

95 96 97 98 99 00 01 02 03—10 9 8 7 6 5 4

To my family, who have supported, encouraged, and loved me. I could never do this if you did not "fan into flame the gift of God" in me.

(II Timothy 1:6)

ACKNOWLEDGMENTS

I would like to thank three people without whom this book would not be possible.

My wife, Karen, corrected and edited the manuscript. Many times, it took great effort on her part to drag some meaning out of what I was saying. I would still be making corrections if it weren't for her.

Jane Rohlin typed the manuscript. The worst part for her was trying to sort through my handwritten notes. I'm still not sure whether my handwriting is worse then my typing.

Cindy LaRusch recorded and transcribed some of the sermons contained in this book, and many that are not. And she stuck to the task to the end! These were the seeds of what is in this book.

ABOUT THE AUTHOR

The Reverend R. Douglas Reinard was born and raised in Aliquippa, Pennsylvania. He was very active in his church during his youth and teen years.

He graduated from Sterling College in Sterling, Kansas, with a B.A. in Bible and Philosophy, and received an M.Div. degree from Eastern Baptist Theological Seminary in Philadelphia.

He has been a pastor for almost twenty years. For the past thirteen years, he has served as pastor of the North Warren Presbyterian Church in North Warren, Pennsylvania.

He lives in North Warren with his wife, Karen, and their two sons, Aaron and Jeremie.

CONTENTS

INTRODUCTION

I have had a lot of fun working on this book because I enjoy children so much. And because I enjoy them so much, I try to provide a meaningful time for them each Sunday morning. And it takes some work on my part to make that happen.

I get to know each child by name. I learn about their family situations, their hobbies, the sports they like, and what makes each one smile. I engage them in conversation before Sunday school, after worship, and on the street. I make each one feel important, because to me, each one is.

The material in this book is not presented to help you avoid the work necessary to have a meaningful time with your children. Instead, it is provided as a help to you. Bend and shape the examples to fit your situation and meet the needs of the children you work with. Use your imagination, hobbies, interests, and skills to venture forth on your own.

But please, do not forget to spend those precious moments outside of worship with the children. The rewards are great. Maybe your office door will become covered with pictures and posters, as mine is. Or maybe a child will make you a simple cross or card to brighten your day. Nothing can compare with being unanimously elected by one child to the high honor of World's Greatest Pastor.

Even without a reward, though, it is worth all the effort you can put forth to help usher these young ones into God's great kingdom. Go for it! "Let the little children come to me, and do not hinder them, for the kingdom of God belongs to such as these" (Mark 10:14*b*).

R. Douglas Reinard

WE CAN SEE GOD'S POWER AND LOVE

MYSTERY BOX OBJECT: Seashell

THEME: By enjoying nature, we understand God better.

SCRIPTURE: For since the creation of the world God's invisible qualities—his eternal power and divine nature—have been clearly seen, being understood from what has been made, so that men are without excuse.—Romans 1:20

LESSON: We have a lake shell in our box today. You say it is not a lake shell—that it is a seashell? We call items like this seashells because we most generally find them by the sea or ocean.

But I have also found seashells on the shores of some large lakes. I found some tiny shells on the shores of Lake Erie and the Sea of Galilee, which is a large lake. So in a way, there can be lake shells.

The strangest place I ever found seashells, though, was in sand dunes in the state of Kansas. Kansas is in the middle of the United States, and it has no oceans or large natural lakes where seashells could come from. And yet, just east of where I attended college in Kansas, you can find small seashells in the sand.

Can you guess why the shells are there? You think someone took them there? That sounds like a good idea, but it is not the answer. Does anyone else have an idea? No?

Well, here is the answer. A long time ago, part of Kansas, which is now far from the sea, was covered by an ocean. Where the eastern shore of that ocean was, you can now find small seashells.

I'm not sure why that ocean was there or why it disappeared. But I am sure that our world is continually changing. Mountains are being worn down by wind and water. River and creek beds are deepening or changing course. God is constantly active, all around us.

In Romans, the apostle Paul tells us that we can see God's power and love just by looking at the things in nature around us. Finding seashells far from the ocean, seeing a stream that has changed course, watching flowers bloom, or feeling grass tickle our toes—all these things help us to understand that God loves us. I hope that today or sometime this week, you can enjoy a tree or a flower, or some other part of nature, because when you do that, you are enjoying God's love.

PRAYER: God, we thank you for loving us and for giving us such a beautiful world in which to live. Help us to take good care of our world, so that others can see your love also.

SOME THINGS WE DO CAN HURT PEOPLE

MYSTERY BOX OBJECT: Civil War hat, Civil War toy pistol, or picture of a cannon.

THEME: God wants us to imitate Jesus.

SCRIPTURE: You became imitators of us and of the Lord; in spite of severe suffering, you welcomed the message with the joy given by the Holy Spirit. And so you became a model to all the believers in Macedonia and Achaia.—I Thessalonians 1:6-7

LESSON: These items from the Civil War in our country remind me of a particular battle in that war, the Battle of Gettysburg, which took place in a small town in south-central Pennsylvania. It was a vicious three-day battle, in which thousands from both the Southern and the Northern armies were killed.

Do you think that maybe some people who were not soldiers could have been killed too? Well at least one person who was not a soldier was killed. Her name was Jennie Wade. She was killed when a bullet came through the wall of her house while she was making bread.

She wasn't fighting. She wasn't on the battlefield. She was minding her own business, and yet she was killed by a stray bullet. Do you think that is fair? It may not be fair, but many innocent people can be hurt when someone does something wrong. If someone is drinking and driving a car, they could have an accident and hurt innocent people. If you play a dirty trick on a friend, that friend could be hurt.

Just as the bad things we do can hurt people, the good things we do can help people. Paul told the people in Thessalonica that their faith and good deeds had been a good example for the people around them. If you do something good, you can help other people, and at the same time, you can show others the good things that need done.

PRAYER: God, help us to do good things for other people. Help us to be more like Jesus, so that we can be a good example to people who do not know you.

GOD WANTS US TO LOVE, NOT FIGHT

MYSTERY BOX OBJECT: Civil War hat, Civil War toy pistol, or a picture of a cannon.

THEME: People who love God will love other people.

SCRIPTURE: This is how we know who the children of God are and who the children of the devil are: Anyone who does not do what is right is not a child of God; nor is anyone who does not love his brother.—I John 3:10

LESSON: These items are reminders of a great war that was fought in our country many years ago. We were not fighting another country. We were fighting among ourselves. That war was called the Civil War, and it was fought between the states in the South and the states in the North.

One of the most unusual things about the Civil War was that many times, members of the same family were fighting against each other. Some fathers and sons fought against each other. Two brothers might serve in different armies and shoot at each other.

Do any of you ever fight with your brothers and sisters? I hope it doesn't happen very often, but in most homes, sisters and brothers fight every once in awhile. My sister and I used to fight all the time when we were young. Sometimes she and I would do nasty things to each other. I'm not proud of the way we treated each other.

For Bev and me, a change came when I was in the seventh grade and she was in twelfth. Both of us were growing to love Jesus more and more, and the more we loved Jesus, the harder it was to fight with each other. That was 31 years ago, and she and I have not had a fight since that time. I love her and her family because Jesus has taught me how to love.

In Galatians 3:28, Paul says, "There is neither Jew nor Greek, slave nor free, male nor female," brother nor sister, mother nor father, "for you are all one in Christ Jesus." God loves your brother or sister or mother or father or neighbor or friend just as much as he loves you. And if God loves all of them, we should also.

Wars and fights begin many times because people won't take the time to realize that God loves other people just as he loves us. And if we love God, we need to love others. In chapter 3 of First John, we are told that if we don't love one another, we are not doing the things God wants us to do. As we love God more, we also need to love others more. That is the way we can stop fighting and wars.

PRAYER: Lord, some of us have been fighting recently. Show us that it is much better to love people than to fight with them. Give us all an opportunity to make up with someone we have fought with recently. Amen.

WE NEED ONE ANOTHER

MYSTERY BOX OBJECT: Tackle box with fishing equipment in it.

THEME: Christians need other Christians for help and support.

SCRIPTURE: But if we walk in the light, as he is in the light, we have fellowship with one another.—I John 1:7

LESSON: This blue metal box is a fishing-tackle box. Inside the box are lots of items to help with fishing. Let's look at some of them. Here is some extra fishing line. And here are some sinkers to weigh down the line so it doesn't float. I also have plenty of lures, including these fake worms. There are quite a lot of things inside here, aren't there?

Do you think I could catch a fish without all these things in my tackle box? I could dig up a live worm and put it on my hook and catch a fish. But all these things in my box are to help me catch that fish easier and faster. If I use all these things properly, I should be a better fisherman.

Do you think you could be a Christian without any other Christians around you? You could, but it wouldn't be very easy. When we have other Christians around, some things seem easier. Instead of laughing at our mistakes, they help and encourage us so that we don't make those mistakes again. When someone is unemployed, other Christians help with the bills. When a person is hurt or ill or in the hospital, other Christians are the ones who visit and pray and send cards.

When I was in the hospital a while back, almost all the cards I received were from Christians. That made me feel better. All my visitors were Christians who prayed for me, and that comforted me. And while I was in the hospital, it was Christians who took care of my family by bringing in meals, babysitting Aaron and Jeremie while Karen visited me in the hospital, and giving them a hug when they needed it. I didn't have to worry about my family, because they were well cared for.

Christians did all these wonderful things because they loved my family and me. And they loved us because God loved them through Jesus. And Jesus told us to love one another.

This tackle box doesn't really make me a better fisherman, because I never seem to catch many fish. But you help me to be a better Christian by loving me and helping me do more good things. Life would be much harder without you. Wherever you go, always look for other Christians to help you.

PRAYER: Thank you, Lord, for the other Christians around us who love us and help us because you love them. Show each of us the ways we can help others. Amen.

OTHERS SHOULD SEE GOD

MYSTERY BOX OBJECT: Bicycle reflector

THEME: We should be pointing others toward God, not toward ourselves.

SCRIPTURE: Let your light shine before men, that they may see your good deeds and praise your Father in heaven.

—Matthew 5:16

LESSON: Do you know what this is? It is a reflector. I think it is from a bicycle. Am I right? When we are finished with this, I hope you plan to put it back on your bike.

Why do we put reflectors on a bicycle? Yes, it is a safety device. It helps us to be seen better, especially when it is getting dark. How many of you have these safety devices on your bikes? If any of you don't have them, you need to ask a parent to help you put them on your bike.

A reflector does exactly what its name says. It does not make light. Light directed at the reflector bounces off, or reflects, so that you can be seen.

Jesus tells us in Matthew that we are to be reflectors of God's love. He tells us that we are to show God's love by the way we treat other people. Now, do you think we are to do this so that people will talk about how wonderful we are? Of course not. We do it so that people will come to love God and praise God for the love we show.

When we do a kindness or show love to other persons, they may thank us for it. That is just fine. But we also want them to thank God for giving us love to share. And we want them to come to know God's love too.

PRAYER: We are glad that you love us, Lord. We are glad that you help us to love other people, so that they also will know your love. Help us to be good reflectors. Amen.

I CAN SEE BETTER

MYSTERY BOX OBJECT: Pair of glasses

THEME: By knowing Jesus, we can know God better.

SCRIPTURE: Anyone who has seen me has seen the Father.

—John 14:9*b*

LESSON: Someone must have gotten new glasses, because we have an old pair in the box today. Let's count how many of us wear glasses. Wow! Eleven of us wear glasses—just over half of us! There seem to be so many more people your age wearing glasses than there were when I was your age.

When I got my first pair of glasses, in first grade, the kids made fun of me and called me "four eyes." But those of us who wear glasses can tell you there is nothing funny about wearing glasses. It is serious business. Without our glasses, we cannot see well enough to read a book, tell time, watch TV, and a lot of other things. Our glasses help us to see better. Without them, we have real problems.

A long time ago many people did not understand God. They thought God demanded hard things from them, and when they failed, that God would punish them harshly. They thought God was only for them and no one else. They did not see God very clearly.

God sent Jesus to earth to help us understand, or see God better. Jesus taught us that God loves us and that we should love one another. He taught us that we should share our faith in God with others, as well as all of the things we have learned about God. We are not to keep it to ourselves.

When I try to read without my glasses, everything is blurred and confused. When I try to understand God without knowing Jesus, I also get confused. Jesus helps me to understand God. In the Gospel of John, Jesus says that anyone who has seen him has seen God. When we know and love Jesus, we know and love God.

PRAYER: Thank you, Lord, for giving us your Son, Jesus. We know that he has shown us your love and has taught us to love one another. We know that he leads us to you. Amen.

GOD WANTS US TO BE GOOD CITIZENS

MYSTERY BOX OBJECT: American flag

THEME: We need to obey laws.

SCRIPTURE: Rulers hold no terror for those who do right, but for those who do wrong. Do you want to be free from fear of the one in authority? Then do what is right.—Romans 13:3

LESSON: Look what is in the box today. It is a flag. What kind of flag is this? That's right, it is the United States flag. All the colors and shapes on the flag have meaning to us. How many stripes are there? Thirteen, correct—seven red stripes and six white stripes. And what do the thirteen stripes stand for? They stand for the thirteen original states.

This blue rectangle in the corner is called a field, and it stands for our "new" form of government. By *new*, I mean that it was different from other forms of government when our country began. How many white stars are on the flag, and what do they stand for? Yes, there are fifty stars, and they represent the fifty states.

Our flag did not always look like this flag that I hold in my hand. Once there were only thirteen stars in a circle, because there were only thirteen states. Also, our flag had fifteen stripes at one time. As they added stars for states, they also added stripes. Soon people realized that adding stars was enough, and the flag returned to thirteen stripes.

Most of you attend school and say the Pledge of Allegiance as school begins each day. Do you know what the Pledge of Allegiance means? It is a promise to be true, or loyal, to your country. That is something that God wants also. In our Bible verse today, we find that Paul is telling us that if we are doing the right things and being good citizens, we should not be afraid of the government. God wants us to always do what is right and obey the laws. When we obey the laws, or rules, in our homes, everything goes well. Christians should also obey our country's laws.

PRAYER: God, help us to obey the rules in our homes and in our country, so that we can be the people you want us to be.

JESUS LEADS US TO GOD'S KINGDOM

MYSTERY BOX OBJECT: American flag

THEME: We belong to the kingdom of God.

SCRIPTURE: But Jesus called the children to him and said, "Let the little children come to me, and do not hinder them, for the kingdom of God belongs to such as these. I tell you the truth, anyone who will not receive the kingdom of God like a little child will never enter it."—Luke 18:16-17

LESSON: We have an American flag in the box today. Where do you see American flags flying or hanging? At school, at the court house, at Memorial Park, and at your home. There is an American flag very close to you. Yes, that is correct. There is one right here in the sanctuary. We have an American flag over by the organ.

Over by the piano, there is another flag. Does anyone know what kind of a flag that is? Yes, it is the Christian flag. Let me hold it out for you so you can see what it looks like.

We have looked at the American flag before and explained the meaning of the colors, the stars, and the stripes. We will do the same with the Christian flag.

The flag reminds us that Jesus did not sin. It also reminds us that if we ask God to forgive us, God will take all our sins away.

The blue field reminds us of part of God's creation, the blue sky. The Bible tells us that Jesus was present with God when the world was created.

The red cross on the blue field reminds us that Jesus died on a cross for us. In Jesus' time, the cross was an ugly thing. Today it is beautiful, because it reminds us of Jesus' love.

The gold trim and tassel remind us that Jesus is the King of kings. And he wants to be the king of our lives, so that we can know his love.

There is even a Pledge of Allegiance to the Christian flag. It goes like this:

> I pledge allegiance to the Christian flag,
> and to the Savior for whose kingdom it stands,
> one fellowship, uniting all Christians
> in service and in love.

We are Americans, but we are also citizens of God's kingdom. Jesus came to earth to announce God's kingdom and to invite everyone to be a part of it. You are at the perfect age to become part of this great kingdom. Does anyone know how you can become part of God's kingdom? By believing in Jesus as the Son of God. Our scripture tells us that the kingdom belongs to you.

PRAYER: Dear Lord, receive these children into your kingdom by their faith in Jesus. Help their teachers and parents to lead them and teach them. But always give them a child's heart of faith.

GOOD OR BAD?

MYSTERY BOX OBJECT: Irish flute or other simple instrument, a piece of music, and a stone.

THEME: The way we use things determines whether they are good or bad.

SCRIPTURE: The voice spoke to him a second time, "Do not call anything impure that God has made clean."—Acts 10:15

LESSON: Would you like to hear me play this flute? Most of you said yes, but I heard a few say no. Why did you say no? Are you afraid that I can't play this flute? Do you think it would sound terrible? Well, you are correct. If I tried to play this flute, it would sound terrible because I do not know how to play it.

But what would happen if I took lessons and practiced? Do you think that I could then play good music? I probably could play better, but whether it would be good music would depend on what kind of music I played. Some of you might like my music, and others might not.

What about this stone? Is it good, or is it bad? Most of you think it is bad. But Benjamin has the right idea: The stone is just a stone; it is neither good nor bad. It is what we do with it that makes it good or bad.

Let me tell you some different ways this stone could be used, and after each statement, you tell me if the use is good or bad. I could use this stone with others to fix a hole in the road. Good. I could use this stone to help make a path. Good. We could make a border around a garden. Good. I could hit someone on the head with it. Bad. I could throw this at a window. Bad. You see, it is what I do with this stone that determines whether it is good or bad.

Most of the things we have are neither good or bad. It is how we use those things that brings out goodness or badness. Music can be bad if we add dirty words to the song, or if we sing or play out of tune. Stones can be bad if we hurt someone with them. But both music and stones can also be good.

You and I must always choose how we are going to use things. We can use them for good purposes or for bad purposes. But I know that God has given us all things to use wisely, for good purposes. Think about the next stone you pick up, and about how you can use it for good.

PRAYER: God, help us to make good choices about how to use the things you have given us. We want to make wise choices, but we need your help. Amen.

24

HOW ARE YOU GROWING?

OBJECT: Baby picture

THEME: God wants us to grow in several ways.

SCRIPTURE: And Jesus grew in wisdom and stature, and in favor with God and men.—Luke 2:52

LESSON: Look at this picture of a cute baby. Is this a picture of you when you were a baby? This sure is a nice picture. How many of you have a picture of yourself when you were a baby? All of you?

How many of you remember when you were a newborn like the one in the photo? No one seems to remember. I don't remember when I was a newborn, either. But I do remember when many of you were first born. What a joy it has been to watch you grow up!

We all know that the Bible tells about Jesus' birth. But do you remember what the Bible tells us about the time he visited the Temple with Mary and Joseph? At the end of that visit, we are told that Jesus kept increasing in stature. He kept growing up.

All of you started out as tiny little babies, and you have been growing up. Once you were little babies, crying during my sermons, and now you are old enough and big enough to be here listening to me.

The scripture also said that Jesus kept increasing in wisdom. *Knowledge* is different from *wisdom*. *Knowledge* is made up of the things you learn. *Wisdom* is knowing how to use all the things you have learned. You may learn a lot about the environment, but you are using wisdom when you begin to recycle, plant trees, and conserve energy. I know you are learning many things. And I also hope you are increasing in wisdom.

The third thing the Scripture says of Jesus is that he increased in favor with God. This means that God was pleased because Jesus was doing what God wanted him to do. Are you pleasing God by doing what he wants you to do?

If we don't take care of ourselves and eat properly, we might not grow to our full potential. If we don't use the things we have learned, we will never have wisdom. And if we don't learn about God and his Son, Jesus, read our Bibles, and pray, we will not grow to please God, because we will not know what God wants us to do.

No one wants to stay a tiny baby. We should not want to be spiritual babies, either. God wants us to grow up.

PRAYER: Dear God, these children are growing so fast, and they need your help. Help them to use in wise ways all the things they are learning in school, at home, and at the church. And help them to grow in their love for you through Jesus. Amen.

YOU NEED A KEY TO UNLOCK THE DOOR

OBJECT: A ring of keys and an old well-worn Bible

THEME: The Bible is our key to open the door to God.

SCRIPTURE: Trust in the Lord and do good; . . .
Delight yourself in the Lord
and he will give you the desires of your heart.
—Psalm 37:3*a*, 4

LESSON: (*Hold up the ring of keys.*) Do you know what these are for? Yes, they are to lock or unlock doors. But do you know what doors they unlock? Of course you don't, but I do. This first key is for my office. The second key is for the secretary's office. And this key is for the outside doors of the church. The last key is for my house.

I have also brought a Bible. This is my Bible now, but originally it belonged to my grandmother. When my grandmother died, the family felt that I should have it. Look how worn it is. The leather cover is falling apart, and some of the pages are loose.

This Bible is like a key. First of all, it was a key for my grandmother to open the door to God. She read this Bible faithfully, and her reading led her closer to God. Without the things she believed and learned in this Bible, she probably would not have been a Christian.

These keys are of no value if I never use them. But when I pull them out of my pocket and put one in a locked door, it is of great use. Your Bible is of no value to you unless you open it and read it. Your Bible is a key that will help you understand God and yourself better.

While looking through this Bible, I noticed that it would open automatically to a passage that my grandmother had underlined. Let me read these two verses to you (*Read Ps. 37:3, 4*). This Bible helped my grandmother trust in the Lord. And if you use your Bible, it will help you trust the Lord also.

PRAYER: Thank you, Lord, for the Bible. Help us to be more faithful in reading it. Help us to trust you more as we read your Word. Amen.

CHILDREN HAVE A SPECIAL PLACE

OBJECT: Railroad spikes

THEME: We all have a special place in the church.

SCRIPTURE: Don't let anyone look down on you because you are young, but set an example for the believers in speech, in life, in love, in faith and in purity.—I Timothy 4:12

LESSON: Does anyone know what this is? (*Hold up one spike.*) Yes, it is a railroad spike. Do you know what a railroad spike does? No? It holds the metal rails to the wooden tie of the railroad track, so that the rails don't move apart when a train passes over them.

I brought along two other spikes, and as you can see, each one is a different size. Can you guess why railroad spikes would come in different sizes? (*Take answers.*) These spikes are different sizes because they have different jobs.

This big long one is used at a switch, where a train can go in either of two directions. A switch has to stand up to heavy work, so the spike needs to be big and heavy. The middle-sized one is from a straight piece of track. It needs to be big and strong, but not nearly as big as the first, because its job is lighter. And the smallest spike comes from a logging railroad of many years ago. Those railroads were set up only long enough to get the cut logs out of the forest. Small spikes were used because they would need to work for only a short period of time.

So there was a different size for each job. No one of these spikes is more important than the others. If any one spike failed to do its job, the train would wreck. All of them are important.

Sometimes in the church, people of your age feel unimportant. That is not right. Just because your size or age is different from that of older members, it doesn't mean that you are less valuable. You may be little spikes, but you have important tasks to do.

One of your tasks is to learn about God, who loves us all so much that he gave us his Son, Jesus. We all need to know that to be saved. Another task is to help lead us in worship when you sing in the children's choir. You make worship so exciting when you sing about your love for Jesus. And there is a third big task you need to do: You need to teach us adults to smile more. When we come to church, our faces look as if we are being tortured. Teach us to smile and be happy that God loves us.

PRAYER: I thank you, Lord, for all these wonderful children. I thank you that they are different from adults and that they have different tasks in this church. Help all of us to remember that even as little spikes, they have important jobs. Amen.

YOU ARE THE TEMPLE OF GOD

OBJECT: Coffee mug

THEME: God wants us to take care of our bodies.

SCRIPTURE: Don't you know that you yourselves are God's temple and that God's Spirit lives in you? If anyone destroys God's temple, God will destroy him; for God's temple is sacred, and you are that temple.—I Corinthians 3:16-17

LESSON: How could you use this mug? Of course, you can use it for drinking. I'm sure we could find other uses, but the primary use would be for drinking. What would you drink out of it? You could drink coffee out of it. That would make it a coffee mug. What else might you drink out of it? Tea, or maybe hot cocoa. So this mug could be used to drink good things, couldn't it?

Could it be used to drink things that are bad for you? It sure could! I know that you are learning in school, at home, and here at church about many of those bad things, and what they do to your body and mind. But you also need to know why Christians, too, believe that those things are bad.

God tells us that our bodies are God's temples. Now, you wouldn't come into the church and throw garbage around, would you? That's right! No way! So if God lives in you, would you throw garbage into your body? God wants us to put good things into our bodies and minds. That means we should eat and drink only good things. It also means we should watch good TV shows and movies, listen to good music, and read good books and magazines. Some of the stuff we can see, hear, or read is garbage also.

How do you learn to tell the good from the bad? Ask your parents and Sunday school teachers. They will always help you to make good choices.

PRAYER: God, protect your lambs. Help them to learn the good things and keep your temples free of garbage. We also pray that you would help the adults of this congregation to be good examples to these young people. Amen.

WHO HAS A PERFECT LIFE?

OBJECT: Picture of a sport, movie, or TV star

THEME: There has been only One who was perfect.

SCRIPTURE: Christ, a lamb without blemish or defect.

—I Peter 1:19*b*

LESSON: How many of you would like to be a sports star, or a TV or movie star? Several of you. Maybe there is something else you would like to be?

It is easy for us to look at well-known people and think about how wonderful their lives must be. They have lots of money to buy anything they want. They have many friends. Their jobs and lives seem so glamorous and wonderful. Many of us think that it would be nice to be such a person.

But you cannot see their whole lives. Many of those famous people are not as happy as you might think. In fact, some of them are quite unhappy. And all of them have problems.

We like to think that they live perfect lives, however. We may even think they are perfect, but there has been only one perfect person, and the Bible says that person was Jesus.

Jesus didn't talk back to his mother, nor did he ever take his friends' toys. He never cheated on a test or fought with the kids down the street. It's not that he wasn't tempted to do those things. He just never gave in to temptation.

All of us are tempted. You and I are tempted, as well as movie stars and sports heroes. Our problem is that we give in to that temptation. We do those bad things that God wants us not to do. Jesus was just like us, except that he didn't do those bad things. God wants us to be without sin, like Jesus was. And we know that we cannot stay away from sin unless God helps us. We cannot be good all the time. Let's ask God to help us.

PRAYER: Lord, we try to be good; but we can't seem to be good all the time. We promise that we will be good, and then we break our promise. We cannot be good without your help. Please help us to try to be more like Jesus. Amen.

POWER UP!

OBJECT: Battery

THEME: Power comes from God through the indwelling Spirit.

SCRIPTURE: "I am going to send you what my Father has promised; but stay in the city until you have been clothed with power from on high."—Luke 24:49

LESSON: Kate has brought a battery in the box today. Have any of you ever seen a battery like this in your home? Well, all of you have. What do we use a battery for? (*Take answers.*) Yes, a remote-control car. A tape player. A computer game. A smoke detector.

A battery looks like a small metal tube. How can a small metal tube make a remote-control car run? How can it make a radio work? You are right! The answer is on the inside of the metal tube. There is energy stored up on the inside. It can be stored in several ways, but the important thing is that it is there, even if we can't see it.

Jesus promised his disciples that they would receive power. The power he was talking about was the Holy Spirit of God. When the disciples received the Holy Spirit on Pentecost, they still looked like fishermen and tax gatherers. Their outer appearance did not change.

But on the inside, they were completely different. When Jesus was crucified, they were very frightened. They were afraid of being arrested or killed. But now, with the Holy Spirit, they became very brave. They bravely and boldly told others about Jesus. They were no longer afraid.

Jesus' promise to the disciples is also a promise to us. We also can receive the power of the Holy Spirit to bravely and boldly tell others about Jesus. The Holy Spirit not only can help us to speak to others about Jesus, but he also can help us to understand the Bible better when we read it and to pray more continually to God. First, you must believe that Jesus is God's Son and ask him into your life. Then you must ask God for his indwelling Holy Spirit. And then you must wait for the Holy Spirit to come into power.

PRAYER: We thank you for your promise of Holy Spirit power. Help us to believe that it is for us, as well as for our parents. Lord God, give us your Holy Spirit.

SAFETY FIRST

OBJECT: Play tool belt

THEME: God wants us to be safe from sin.

SCRIPTURE: So he called one of the servants and asked him what was going on. "Your brother has come," he replied, "and your father has killed the fattened calf because he has him back safe and sound."—Luke 15:26-27

LESSON: Look at this nice tool belt that Ryan brought in for us. Ryan can wear this and take his tools wherever he goes. And when he is finished using a tool, he can put it back on his belt so that he doesn't lose it. Here he has a hammer, a pair of pliers, a screwdriver, a tape measure, and a small pouch to hold nails, screws, or other small objects.

Do any of you know whether there are any tools in your home? All of you have some, I'm sure. Somewhere in your home, there is a toolbox or drawer where tools are kept. Are you allowed to play with the tools? Yes, but only if there is an adult around to help you use the tools properly and safely.

When I worked in a factory, my boss was always talking to us about using tools safely and working in a safe manner. He didn't want us to be injured. He wanted us to stay healthy so that we could get our work finished.

God also wants us to be safe when we are using tools. I believe that God wants us to be careful so that we will not be injured. God does not want us to be careless or to be in danger.

When we sin, we are in danger. Because once we have sinned, it is much easier to do it again and again. God wants us to stop sinning and ask to be forgiven. The scripture lesson today tells us about a son who went away from home because he wanted to be free of his father and do whatever he wanted to do. The boy wasted his money and ended up hungry. He realized that if he went home, asked for forgiveness, and asked to be a servant, then he would have enough to eat. When he got home and asked for forgiveness, his father welcomed him back—not as a servant, but as a son. And there was a celebration because he was safe again.

God is like the father in the story, and we are like the son. God wants us to receive forgiveness, and be accepted as God's children. God doesn't want us to keep sinning. We need to go to God and ask to be forgiven. Let's ask God in prayer to forgive us and accept us as God's children.

PRAYER: God, we are not always good people. Sometimes we do things that we know you do not want us to do, like fighting or arguing. Forgive us for these things, and help us to know that we are your children. We want to be safe as your children because we love you. Amen.

WHAT KIND OF TOOL ARE YOU?

OBJECT: Play tool belt

THEME: God will use us to do good things.

SCRIPTURE: Let us do good to all people, especially to those who belong to the family of believers.—Galatians 6:10

LESSON: Ryan brought us a tool belt this week. Look at all the tools on this belt. These are play tools, but they are just like the ones your mothers and fathers might use around the house. Here is a hammer for pounding nails. There is also a pair of pliers for holding things.

The purpose of a tool is to help us do a job. Can you imagine trying to pound a nail with your hand? Ouch! A hammer does a better job. Would you try to cut a board with your teeth? No way! You would use a saw to do that job.

Have you ever thought of yourself as a tool? Probably not, but God has. God can do anything he chooses, in any way he chooses. God chooses to use you and me to do good things for others. God could do it without us, but he chooses to use us to do those good things.

If we are God's tools, then we should do as he directs us. How do you think God can use you to do good to others? Tell them about Jesus, yes. Help a neighbor rake leaves. Help your mom and dad around the house. Those are all good ideas.

Some other ideas might be to help a friend with school work, say "I love you" to someone, or offer to do a job around the church. All of these are ways of being God's tools to do good to others.

PRAYER: Lord, we want to be your good tools. Help us to learn to do good things for others without being asked. Amen.

YOU CAN EAT SOME FLOWERS

OBJECT: Nasturtium blossom (or other edible flower)

THEME: If we are faithful in small things, we will be faithful in big things.

SCRIPTURE: "Well done, my good servant!" his master replied. "Because you have been trustworthy in a very small matter, take charge of ten cities."—Luke 19:17

LESSON: Look at the pretty flowers I brought in for you to see. These flowers are called Nasturtiums. We have these growing around our house. I like the way they look. But do you know what I like best about Nasturtiums? (*While the children are answering, pick a few petals and begin to eat them.*) I like to eat Nasturtiums.

Some of you are looking at me as if I am crazy! Don't you eat flowers for dinner? No! Well, to be honest, neither do I.

And let me warn you that most flowers cannot be eaten. In fact, many of them are poisonous. Please never put any flower or plant in your mouth unless a very experienced adult helps you to distinguish the good from the bad.

There are many herbs and plants, besides vegetables, that are good for us. In olden days, people used some of those little plants as medicines. But since most of us do not know which ones they are, they seem unimportant, so we don't pay much attention to them. And not only are we forgetting how to use those little plants, but we are forgetting also about the need for forests.

We want to skip the small things and move on to the big things. But God calls us to first be faithful in taking care of the small things. That means not only in the forest, but also in the church. We can't lead others to Christ until we first come to him.

Jesus tells us that when we have been faithful in small things, God will give us the big things. But if we can't even do the little things, how can we ever handle larger things?

And I want you to remember that you are never to put into your mouth any flower or plant unless a very experienced adult helps you to distinguish the good from the bad. I would never want you to eat something that could harm you.

PRAYER: O Lord, give these children patience to do the small jobs before they move on to the larger jobs. Help them to learn, so that they will be ready to teach. Help them to follow leaders, so they will know how to lead. And help them to accept your Son, Jesus, as Lord, so that they may lead others to him. Amen.

GOD SEEKS THE LOST SHEEP

OBJECT: A ring, or any other object lost at the church

THEME: God rejoices when we receive him.

SCRIPTURE: "Rejoice with me; I have found my lost sheep." I tell you that in the same way there will be more rejoicing in heaven over one sinner who repents than over ninety-nine righteous persons who do not need to repent.—Luke 15:6b-7

LESSON: Look at this pretty ring. Don't you think it looks good on my hand? Danny says it doesn't look good because it's too small, and it looks like a girl's ring. He is right. This ring is too small for my finger, and from the design, it looks like a ring that a girl or woman would own.

Obviously, this is not my ring. Whose ring do you think it is? No, it is not my wife's ring. No, it is neither the church treasurer's nor secretary's. You could guess all day, and I wouldn't even know if you guessed correctly. You see, I don't know whose ring this is. Someone lost it here in the church about a month ago, and we haven't been able to find the owner.

This is a pretty ring. Can you imagine how bad its owner must feel about losing it? Have you ever lost something that meant a lot to you? You wish you could get it back. You feel sad.

God certainly feels sad when any person is lost. By lost, I mean not following God. God is like a shepherd who has lost a sheep. Even though there are ninety-nine sheep that are safe and sound, God continues to try to bring the one lost sheep home. God wants everyone to come to him.

How do you feel when you lose something, and then find it again? Right—really excited! The Bible says that the heavens rejoice when we turn to God and seek forgiveness through Jesus. We can help others to turn to God by telling them what we know about Jesus. We can become little shepherds, looking for God's lost sheep.

PRAYER: God, we thank you for all of the sheep that are yours. Help us to find that lost sheep (person) so that we can tell it about you. Then you can rejoice when it is found.

GOD DOES NOT CONTROL OUR LIVES

OBJECT: Marionette

THEME: God does not force us to follow him.

SCRIPTURE: We all, like sheep, have gone astray,
each of us has turned to his own way. . . .
But Christ lives in me.
—Isaiah 53:6*a;* Galatians 2:20*b*

LESSON: Well, look at this cute little fellow. I could enjoy playing with this. Does anyone know what we call this object that Peter has brought in? A puppet? That's close, but there is a special name for this kind of puppet. Yes, a marionette.

Most puppets are operated by placing one or two hands inside the puppet. You move the puppet by moving your fingers, or by moving levers or strings inside the puppet. A marionette, on the other hand, is controlled from the outside. These strings from the legs, arms, and head are attached to these wooden sticks. When you move the sticks, the marionette moves.

As you can see, I am not very skilled at working with marionettes. After much practice, a person could make this marionette walk or wave or bow, or many other things. The person holding these sticks controls all the actions of the marionette.

Some people have the idea that God controls our lives just as a person controls a marionette. They feel that God only has to wiggle a finger, and we will do the things he wants us to do. But I don't believe the Bible tells us that.

God certainly wants us to follow him, but he does not force us to do it. He allows us to choose whether we want to follow him. God does not pull a string which makes us want to follow him.

If God forced us to follow him, it would be very easy to be a Christian. We would not need to make a choice. We would do exactly as God told us. But God wants us to follow him because we love him, not because he has forced us to follow him.

We can make this marionette do what we want it to do by pulling these strings. But it can never do what we want it to do just because it loves us. We can do what God wants us to do because we love God. We can choose to follow God.

PRAYER: We are glad, Father, that you love us. Help us to show our love for you by following you, not because you force us to, but because we choose to follow. Amen.

WHAT TIME IS IT?

OBJECT: Watch or clock

THEME: It is time for each of us to make a decision.

SCRIPTURE: Choose for yourselves this day whom you will serve . . . . But as for me and my household, we will serve the Lord.—Joshua 24:15

LESSON: I am sure that everyone knows what this object is. It is a watch. And it is used to tell the temperature, right? No, it is used to tell us what time it is. By looking at this watch, you can tell me what time it is? That's right, it is 2:27 A.M. Wait a minute! It can't be 2:27 A.M., because the sun is shining. I think this watch must be wrong. Do you agree with me?

So we really can't tell what time it is with this watch. If we needed to be someplace at 11:30, we would be late if we trusted this watch. In fact, we would never know the exact time. We could only guess what the correct time is.

Have you ever been asked to do something, and you said, "I'll do it later?" And after a few hours had passed, you were reminded that the task was not complete, and you said, "I'll do it before I go to bed"? But when bedtime came, you still had not done what you were asked to do? You had run out of time.

We have the same problem in our spiritual lives. We say, "Tomorrow I am going to start reading the Bible," or, "I need to start having a prayer time each day." But many times, we only talk about it; we never do it. We run out of time. Instead of our time with God being first, it comes last, if we do it at all.

Many people run into the same problem when it comes to accepting Jesus as their Lord and Savior. They keep saying they will do it later. But just as with your chores, later never seems to come. So they put off making that very important decision.

Joshua told the people to "choose this day." Joshua knew that this is an important decision that should not be delayed. Joshua led by example, for he told the people that he and his family had decided to follow the Lord.

With this watch, we may never know the right time. But with God, we know that any time is the correct time to read the Bible, or to pray, or to receive Jesus.

PRAYER: Please help these young children to come to an early decision about serving you, Father. Even as they are just learning to tell time, help them to learn the important lessons of salvation in Jesus. Amen.

I'M AFRAID

OBJECT: Halloween mask or something scary

THEME: God wants us to understand and not to be afraid.

SCRIPTURE: Then Jesus said to them, "Do not be afraid."
—Matthew 28:10a

LESSON: Look at this ugly mask. This seems like a strange time of year to have a mask in the box. Today I would have expected a chocolate rabbit, or an egg.

This mask probably doesn't scare any of you now, while I am holding it here in church. But if I were wearing it on a dark night, you might be frightened. You would be frightened because you wouldn't know whose face was under the mask, and because things seem different in the dark. Also, sometimes we are frightened by things we do not understand.

When the women went to the tomb to find the body of Jesus, they found the tomb empty. They did not understand that. As they were returning, they saw Jesus, who had died on the cross. They couldn't understand that either, because dead people don't walk. And they must have been afraid, because Jesus told them not to be afraid.

I think I might have been frightened too, if I had been there. Do you think you would have been afraid?

When we think about it, there was nothing to be afraid of. Jesus was alive. And now we know that we should be excited and full of joy, not fear. Easter is a time of celebration for Christmas. We celebrate because Jesus is alive, and because we have a wonderful message for people who live in fear.

Have you ever been afraid of a mask, or the dark, or a loud noise, or something you did not understand? Most of us have been afraid at some time in our lives. Well, the resurrection—Jesus rising from the dead—is one event we do not need to be afraid of, even if we do not understand it. It is one of the many ways God tells us that he loves us. And just as he told the women that morning not to be afraid, he reminds us, through Easter, not to be afraid.

PRAYER: Sometimes it is easy for us to be afraid, Lord, especially when we are young. Be with these children and help them not to be afraid. Amen.

ON THE BEACH

OBJECT: Sand

THEME: We know Jesus by what he does.

SCRIPTURE: Early in the morning, Jesus stood on the shore, but the disciples did not realize that it was Jesus.—John 21:4

LESSON: I have a small bag of sand in the box today. How many of you like to play in the sand? All of you. What do you like to play in the sand? I should have guessed. Most of you like to build sandcastles. That is a lot of fun.

When I was a young boy, a friend of mine took two large boards and carved big, ugly footprints on one side of each board. He tied these on his shoes and walked on a sandy beach near here. He hoped that people would see the big, ugly footprints and think that some strange animal had been there. Several of us saw the footprints in the sand, but we knew they were not made by an animal. We knew that our friend, who liked to play jokes, was the footprint maker. We recognized his work.

One night after Jesus rose from the dead, the disciples went fishing. Early in the morning, as they were coming into shore, they saw a man standing on the shore, but they could not tell who it was. Maybe they were too far out in the water, or maybe it was foggy that early in the morning. But whatever the reason, they did not recognize Jesus.

Jesus called out to the fishermen and asked if they had caught anything. They said they hadn't, so Jesus told them to throw their nets on the other side of the boat. They still did not know who he was, but they did what he said, and immediately, they caught so many fish that the nets were too heavy to pull into the boat.

At that point, John recognized Jesus. How do you think John knew it was Jesus? (*Wait for answers.*) Well, I doubt if John knew it was Jesus because he could see his face. I think it was because he knew the kinds of things Jesus did. John knew that only Jesus, who had fed five thousand people with five loaves and two fish, could fill a net so full of fish.

I'll bet that you would know Jesus by the things he would do. Would Jesus heal blind people? Would Jesus talk to children? Would Jesus cheat on a test? See, you would know Jesus by the things he would do.

If you say that you are a follower of Jesus, then people should be able to see that you are a Christian by the things you do. If we follow Jesus, we will do good things, like he did, and people will know that we are Christians.

PRAYER: Lord, when we play in the sand, remind us about the morning Jesus stood on the shore. Remind us also to be more like Jesus, so that people will know that we follow Jesus. Amen.

GOD PREPARED A PLACE FOR JESUS

OBJECT: Straw or hay

THEME: Just as God planned the birth of Jesus, so he has plans for us.

SCRIPTURE: She wrapped him in cloths and placed him in a manger.—Luke 2:7b *(After the sermon, sing "Away in a Manger.")*

LESSON: The box is full of straw today. This straw is scratchy. If you rubbed some on your arm or back, it wouldn't feel very good. It might even make you itch.

How would you like to sleep on some straw? Most of you don't think it would be fun. But straw would make a soft bed, if you prepared it properly. If you covered some straw with a big blanket and slept on the blanket, you would have a soft bed.

When you think of baby Jesus sleeping, what do you think of? A manger, yes. Does anyone know what a manger is? It is a feeding trough for animals. When Jesus was placed in a feeding trough to sleep, do you think Mary and Joseph might have made the bed softer with some straw or hay? It could be.

A bed of straw in a feeding trough doesn't seem like such a great place for God's Son. A fancy bed in a big palace is the place most of us would choose for Jesus' first bed. But God had a much different plan. God planned for Jesus to be born in a stable on a bed of straw, so that shepherds and sick people and children would feel good about coming to him. They would have been afraid of a king.

The king at that time was a very cruel man. The people would not have trusted anyone born in the king's palace. Besides, the king would have killed Jesus, as he tried to do after the visit of the Magi (wise men).

God had a good plan. He always does. He even has a good plan for your life, as he does for mine. As we grow, God shows us a little bit of the plan at a time. You must pray and ask God to show you what good things he has for you. And then, knowing how good his plan was for Jesus' birth, it becomes easier to follow where he leads.

Straw may not seem like very good material to make a bed, but remember, God had a plan.

PRAYER: We know that we can trust you, Lord. Begin to show these young people your loving plans for their lives. And help them to trust you enough to follow you. Amen.

DID YOU INHERIT YOUR FAITH?

OBJECT: Camera

THEME: Just because a parent is a Christian, it doesn't mean that the child is a Christian.

SCRIPTURE: I have been reminded of your sincere faith, which first lived in your grandmother Lois and in your mother Eunice and, I am persuaded, now lives in you also. . . . Continue in what you have learned and have become convinced of, because you know those from whom you learned.—II Timothy 1:5; 3:14

LESSON: Would anyone like me to take your picture? Only a few of you would like your picture taken. Why don't the rest of you want your picture taken? Are you afraid you will break the camera? Believe me, that is impossible. Besides, I think all of you would look nice in a picture. But I can't take your pictures because Matt didn't put film in the camera.

I was looking through some old pictures of my parents recently when I found a few pictures of one of my grandmothers. It has been a long time since I last looked at pictures of her. Just seeing those pictures brought many memories to my mind. I remember how proud she was that God had called me to be a pastor. I remember that when she sang, she was more concerned about singing with joy than she was about the tune.

Old pictures can bring back memories. My greatest memory of my grandmothers was of their simple faith in Jesus. My parents, in time, received Jesus as their Savior. When my sister and I were in our teens, we also accepted Jesus. But I didn't automatically become a Christian because a grandparent or parent was a Christian. Each of us must decide for ourselves to accept Jesus.

Paul reminds Timothy of the faith of his grandmother and mother. Then he tells Timothy to continue in his own faith because of what he had learned and become convinced of. A Christian parent, grandparent, or friend can help us learn about Jesus, but no one can accept him for us. We must do that for ourselves.

I know that some of you have already accepted Jesus as your Lord and Savior. And that is the most important decision you will ever make. Maybe some others of you are ready to make that decision today. If you are ready, pray silently with me.

PRAYER: Dear God, I am a sinner. No matter how hard I try, I still do wrong things. I know that your Son, Jesus, died and rose again so that my sins would be forgiven. I believe in Jesus and ask him into my heart. Thank you that he is inside me now. Amen.

IT IS EASY TO FORGET

OBJECT: Camera

THEME: Jesus tells us to remember him.

SCRIPTURE: "This cup is the new covenant in my blood;
do this . . . in remembrance of me."
—I Corinthians 11:25*b*

LESSON: This is a nice camera, Matt. Is it yours? It is! I can imagine that you take good pictures with it.

How many of you have cameras? Well, quite a few of you do. My first camera was an old used box camera that my sister didn't want any more. And the pictures I took with it looked old and used also!

I like old pictures—especially old pictures of myself and my family. When I see those pictures, it brings back memories of the time when I was your age. I can remember the house I lived in and the friends I played with. I can even remember the secret place where I hid things in my closet.

Remembering all those things is good. As you get older, you will store up more and more memories, and old photographs are a way of opening the door to those stored memories.

Today in our worship, we will be celebrating what we call the Lord's Supper. It can also be called Communion, or the Eucharist. We will drink little cups of wine (*grape juice*) and eat little pieces of bread (*wafers*). Does anyone know why we do this? Yes, because Jesus did it with his disciples. And because Jesus told us to do it to remember him.

Like a photograph, the Lord's Supper reminds us of Jesus and what he did for us on the cross. We are reminded that he died for our sins. We are also reminded that he rose again from death to show us that, through him, we can live forever.

Listen closely when I read the scripture, just before the serving of the bread, and count the number of times I read the word *remembrance*. And then remember Jesus.

PRAYER: It is good to remember what your Son, Jesus, did for us on the cross. Help us to remember him and to remember your love for us. Amen.

WE NEED TO BE HELPERS

OBJECT: A travel game

THEME: We can get into trouble when we have nothing to do.

SCRIPTURE: And we urge you, brothers, warn those who are idle, encourage the timid, help the weak, be patient with everyone.
—I Thessalonians 5:14

LESSON: In the box today, there is a fun travel game for me to play with. Do you think anyone would mind if I played with this game during church? You do think they would mind. I guess you are right. I can imagine that the choir might be upset if I were playing with this while they were praising God.

Well, if church is not a good place to play a travel game, I can think of a good place. How about in a car, while you are traveling on a vacation or going to visit your grandparents? Maybe that is why it is called a travel game.

Let me ask you some serious questions. While you were traveling, have any of you asked your parents, "Are we almost there?" Almost all of you admit to having asked that question. How many of you have ever fought with a brother or sister while you were on a trip? And how many of you, while traveling, have ever complained that you are bored? Almost all of you.

Did you know that all those things get on your parents' nerves? And they can also be a great bother to the driver, when the traffic is heavy or the roads are bad. You are not being helpers to your parents.

But there is a way you can be helpers. You can keep yourselves and maybe a brother or sister busy by playing a travel game such as this, or by making up a game. It helps to make the trip seem shorter, and it helps your moms and dads enjoy the trip more.

When I was young, my sister and I would make up our games, because we didn't have travel games then. We would count gas stations, each of us choosing one side of the highway. When either of us saw a junkyard, we would lose all our gas stations and have to begin counting all over again. It was fun, and it kept us out of trouble.

In today's scripture, Paul warns us against being idle. That means having nothing to do. When we have nothing to do we usually get into trouble or cause problems for others.

We need to keep busy and stay out of trouble, especially on a trip. That way, we can be of great help to others.

PRAYER: Lord, we thank you for travel games and other things that can keep us busy on a trip. And we thank you for the ability to take trips. Help us all to be answers to problems instead of the problems. Amen.

A PRICE HAS BEEN PAID FOR US

OBJECT: Store coupon

THEME: We have been bought with a price.

SCRIPTURE: For he has rescued us from the dominion of darkness and brought us into the kingdom of the Son he loves, in whom we have redemption, the forgiveness of sins.—Colossians 1:13-14

LESSON: Some of you may not know what this piece of paper is. It is called a manufacturer's coupon. If you went to the store to buy the item pictured on this coupon, you would be able to buy it for 20¢ less than the price marked on the item. If the item cost $1.00, the store would charge you only 80¢. When you buy something using a coupon, it is called *redemption*. You use the coupon to *redeem*, or pay part of the purchase price.

The store does not lose the 20¢ when you use this coupon. The store gives it to the people who made the product, and they give the 20¢ back to the store. The people who made the product do all this so that you will buy what they make. If you like the product, you will buy more of it, and they will make money.

The Bible talks about redemption—buying back—only the Bible does not talk about coupons. Instead, the Bible talks about God's love, our sins, and the death of Jesus, when it talks about "buying back."

God loved Adam and Eve when he created them, but they sinned; they did what God told them not to do. They turned away from God's love. Many times, God had tried to show people that he loved them, but most people kept on sinning and being bad. Finally, God sent his Son, Jesus, to show us God's love.

Jesus was able to show us God's love as he taught and healed people. But he did more than that. He bought us back by taking all our sins upon himself when he died on the cross. A coupon pays part of the price of a product, but Jesus paid everything we owe for the bad things we do.

PRAYER: When we look at the cross, remind us of your love for us. Remind us that Jesus died because of our sins. And help us to know that because he rose from the dead, we will have life with you forever. Amen.

WHAT DO PASTORS DO?

OBJECT: Clergy stole, picture of pastor, or something else associated with a pastor.

THEME: A pastor can have many jobs in the church, but one of them is especially important.

SCRIPTURE: And pray for each other so that you may be healed.—James 5:16*b*

LESSON: Do any of you know what this is that I am holding? You are right. It is the thing I wear sometimes in church. But do you know what it is called? No one has an answer? Well, it is called a stole, and many pastors wear them during worship.

I brought this stole in the box so that I would remember to tell you two short stories. The first story is about a young boy. One day while my wife and I were eating in a restaurant, we saw a family from the church. The mother asked her young son if he knew who I was.

He said, "He's God." I heard you laugh! It is funny. I am not God.

The second story is about my own son, who said he wanted to be a pastor because all I ever did was eat candy and talk to the church secretary. I heard you laugh again. This story is also funny.

Do any of you know what I do? (*Wait for answers.*) Yes, I preach sermons. I also teach a Sunday school class. Do you know of anything else I do? Well, let me tell you about some of the things I do.

Besides teaching Sunday school, I teach Bible classes at other times during the week. At those classes, we read and try to understand the Bible better. Now, to teach a Bible class and Sunday school, or to preach a sermon, I need to spend a lot of time reading and studying the Bible by myself. I can't teach very well if I don't know anything.

I visit with a lot of people. I visit sick people in the hospital, in the nursing home, or in their own homes. I talk with them, read the Bible to them, and pray with them. I also visit with people who are not sick, but who maybe cannot leave their homes or have had some bad problems. And sometimes I visit people just because they want me to visit with them. Then there are days when I need to write letters or talk on the phone or attend meetings.

But no matter how busy I get, there is one thing that has become very important to me, and I do it every day. Every day, I pray for you. I pray that God will protect you. I pray that through the teaching of your parents and Sunday-school teachers, you will know a lot about God and his Son, Jesus. But mostly, I pray that you will come to love Jesus just as much as he loves you. I want you to always remember that I pray for you every day and that, to me, it is my most important job.

PRAYER: O God, hear my prayer for your children. Guard them and protect them. Help us to teach them. Lead them to love you as you love them. Amen.

MEASURING OUR GROWTH

OBJECT: Tape measure

THEME: As Christians, we need to be serving God.

SCRIPTURE: "Well done, good and faithful servant!"

—Matthew 25:21a

LESSON: Now, what do you think I could do with this thing? (*Hold up tape measure and wait for answers.*) Sure, I can measure things. Stand up and let me measure your height. You are 3 feet, 7 inches tall. My shoe is 11 inches long. My index finger is only 3 inches long. We can use this tape measure to find the length or height of many things.

Do you think we should measure all the feet here in church and see who has the largest? You think that is a good idea! It might be funny to some of us, but I'm afraid that many of the adults might not think it is so funny.

There are other ways of measuring things besides using a tape measure. If you are in a race, you can measure how fast the other racers are, compared to you. Sally may be faster or slower than others. In an art contest, you can measure others by their ability to paint a good picture. Some may have more talent than others.

We can also be measured by the things we do or don't do. If we are always getting into trouble, others will notice that we do not behave as well as we should. But if we are doing good things for others, people will notice that we are behaving very well.

A good way to measure ourselves in the church is to look at Jesus. Would Jesus say nasty things to people? Of course not. If we say nasty things, then we know that we are not doing as well as Jesus. We should always try to be as good as Jesus. We know that we will sometimes fail, but Jesus is the one we should always try to be like.

The man in our scripture lesson sets a good example for us. He did what he was supposed to do. His reward was a compliment for his work. When we do the kinds of things Jesus did, like treating people nicely or taking care of their needs, we are like the faithful servant in the scripture. Wouldn't it be wonderful to hear God tell us that we have done a good job of serving him?

PRAYER: Sometimes it is hard to be young, Lord. We do not always do the right things. Help us all to try to be more like Jesus. Amen.

A TREE'S PRAYER

OBJECT: A small tree planted in a pot.

THEME: God answers our prayers in ways that sometimes surprise us.

SCRIPTURE: And we know that in all things God works for the good of those who love him.—Romans 8:28*a*

LESSON: This is a cute little Maple tree. Did you plant this? You found it growing next to your house and transplanted it into this flower pot?

I can close my eyes and imagine what this tree will look like when it is big. Children will climb up in its branches and play. Birds will build their nests high up near the top. And the tree will grow thousands of seeds, which can grow into more trees.

This little tree reminds me of the story about the three trees that grew on a hillside many years ago. They were big old trees. Now, trees don't think or pray, but in this story, we will pretend that these trees can both think and pray.

The first tree prayed that if it were cut down, its wood would be used to build a palace for a king. In a few years a woodsman came and cut the tree down and made boards from the trunk. But the wood was used to build a stable, not a palace.

The tree felt as if its prayer had not been answered. Why had God used it to make a stable, when it had prayed to be a palace? But a few years later, a baby was born in that stable. That baby's name was Jesus.

The second tree prayed to be made into a wonderful sailing ship that would travel great distances. But when it was cut down, it was made into a simple fishing boat, and it traveled only short distances, carrying stinky fish. God had not answered its prayer.

But one day as its owner was cleaning his nets, a young teacher came along and asked if he could stand in the boat to teach the large crowd. The name of the young teacher was Jesus.

The third tree prayed that it would never be cut down. It wanted to stand on that hillside forever. But it was cut down, so its prayer was not answered either.

The wood from the third tree was used to make a cross. A great teacher was nailed to that cross and died. That great teacher's name was Jesus.

None of the trees received what they had asked for. Instead, what they received was much greater. The first became a simple palace for the King of kings. The second became a platform for some of

Jesus' teachings. And the third still stands today as a sign of God's love.

Have you ever prayed for something you didn't receive? God will answer your prayers, but maybe not in the way you think. God may have something for you that is better than what you prayed for. Trust God to give you all the good things you need.

God has a good plan for this small tree, and he has a good plan for you. Just remember that he may surprise you.

PRAYER: Thank you, O Lord, for hearing our prayers. We also thank you for giving us even greater things than we ask for. Help us to wait for your good answers.

HOOKED

OBJECT: Box of fishhooks

THEME: We need to be careful with things that can hurt us.

SCRIPTURE: Whatever is true, whatever is noble, whatever is right, whatever is pure, whatever is lovely, whatever is admirable—if anything is excellent or praiseworthy—think about such things.—Philippians 4:8

LESSON: Someone must be a fisherman. Look at all these fishhooks. Do you own fishing poles and other fishing equipment? Do you catch many fish? Sometimes?

Do any of the rest of you like to fish? When you go fishing, are you warned to be careful with the hook? Of course, all the time. Why should you be careful with the hook? Well, that's one reason. The hook is very sharp, and it can hurt if you stick yourself with it. But there is another reason. Yes, that's right. The hook also has a barb on it.

The barb is this little piece here. (*Show the children.*) If you stick yourself with a pin, you can easily remove the pin. But if you stick yourself with a fishhook, the barb makes it hard to remove the hook. It is the barb that keeps the hook in the mouth of the fish. Once the barb is in, the fish can't get away easily.

Some things we do in our lives are like barbs. Once we start doing that thing, we cannot easily stop. The thing I am thinking about today is drugs. I know that you have been hearing a lot about drugs this week in school. You have been taught what drugs look like and what they can do to your body.

If you know some older people who use drugs, you may think they look cool. But they are not cool. A person who uses drugs is just like a fish caught on a hook. And if you try drugs, you will be hooked also.

God wants us to keep ourselves pure, free of things like drugs. God never wants us to get hooked, because he knows that would hurt us.

I don't think fish are very smart to get themselves hooked. I know you are much smarter. If someone ever offers you drugs, remember the fish, and remember that God wants you to be pure and free of drugs. Then just walk away.

PRAYER: Lord, you know all about the bad things that are around us. Help us to stay away from things that will get us hooked like a fish. Amen.

COVER UP

OBJECT: Blanket

THEME: It does not take much to help others.

SCRIPTURE: "I needed clothes and you clothed me . . . whatever you did for one of the least of these brothers of mine, you did for me."—Matthew 25:36, 40

LESSON: I have something to show you today that is so big it wouldn't fit in the box. So I put it in a much larger box. What is it? It is a blanket.

You don't seem very excited by this blanket. I thought all of you would be so excited to see a blanket for the first time. What do you mean, you've seen blankets before? Where have you seen a blanket? At home! You must be very lucky to have a blanket in your home. What! You have several blankets at home? You people must be rich!

Did you know that there are many people who do not have even one blanket? Some of those people without blankets are children your own age. It is getting colder as winter comes, and those people are without blankets, while you and I have several blankets. Don't you wish you could share an extra blanket with someone?

Well, you can. The mission committee is collecting money to send blankets to people who don't have them. Your family can help send a blanket to someone who needs it, for just $5.00, less than the cost of a pizza.

At my house, we've already talked it over. We're going to give several gifts of $5.00, to buy several blankets. We think our own blankets will feel warmer this winter if we know we have helped someone else stay warm.

Talk it over in your family. Maybe you and your family would like to help us buy some blankets. Jesus said that when we help others in need, it is as if we were doing it for him.

PRAYER: Thank you, Lord, for nice warm blankets. We know they will keep us warm when it is cold. We pray that we can help others to be as warm as we are. Amen.

FOLLOW THE RULES

OBJECT: A trophy

THEME: Many rules are fun.

SCRIPTURE: This is love for God: to obey his commands. And his commands are not burdensome.—I John 5:3

LESSON: Look at this beautiful trophy that Ben put in the box. It says, "World's Best Pastor." No, it really says, "Mr. Snyder—Coach" on it.

Trophies are given out to people who do a great job in a sport or competition. Seldom will you receive a trophy for playing poorly. And never will you receive one for cheating.

When you play a sport or compete, you follow the rules. In baseball, the rules say that you can run only one way around the bases. You start at home plate and run to first base, then to second base, then to third base, and then back to home. If you run in any other order, you are out. Rules make the game fair, fun, and exciting for everyone.

Do you know of any rules around the church? (*Wait for answers.*) Right. No running. No yelling. Don't steal things. Can you think of anything else? In the kindergarten and nursery rooms, it is a rule that you help put things away.

Who made those rules? No, God didn't make them. Neither did I. I am sure that at some time, someone has told you there is no running in church. But God didn't make that rule. In fact, the only rule that God gave us through Jesus is that we should love one another.

To love one another covers a lot. If I love you, do you think I would steal from you? No, of course not. If I love you, would I play with your toys and leave them scattered all over the floor? No. We do good things for one another—not because we have to, but because God loves us and we love one another. I come in the church and put toys away because I want to—not because a rule tells me I have to. God loves us because he wants to, not because he has to.

PRAYER: Dear God, thank you for loving us. Help us to love one another, and because we love one another, to do good things for others. Amen.

RUN THE RACE

OBJECT: Trophy

THEME: To win, you must practice and work.

SCRIPTURE: Do you not know that in a race all the runners run, but only one gets the prize? Run in such a way as to get the prize.—I Corinthians 9:24

LESSON: This is the trophy Ben received last year for hitting 370 home runs. No, the trophy really says, "Mr. Snyder—Coach," on it, so it must belong to Ben's father. I'm wrong again. Ben says it is his grandfather's trophy.

Do any of you have a trophy? A few of you do. Did you receive the trophy for staying at home and not participating? Of course not. You get a trophy for competing and finishing what you started. You can never win an award if you don't participate fully.

The apostle Paul tells us that living as a Christian is like running a race. Paul says that we should run the race in such a way that we win the prize at the end. In other words, if you are going to be a Christian, you need to practice and work at being the best Christian you can be.

Some people think they can be good Christians by coming to church on Sunday, and then forgetting about God the rest of the week. Do you think you could be a great ballplayer if you played only when you felt like it? You would never win a trophy that way. You can't be a Christian only when you feel like it. Christians try to be the best they can be all the time.

Our reward for constantly trying to serve God the best we can is just the joy of serving God—to know that we have run the race and won.

PRAYER: Help these young children, O God, to run this Christian race. And help us adults to teach them, by word and deed, that to be a Christian is to commit one's life to you. Amen.

DO UNTO OTHERS

OBJECT: Toy wrestler

THEME: God calls us to do good and loving things for one another.

SCRIPTURE: So in everything, do to others what you would have them do to you.—Matthew 7:12

LESSON: How many of you watch wrestling on TV? How many of you think that what you see is real? I've seen wrestlers hit each other over the head with chairs, kick each other in the face, throw each other out of the ring, and walk away with a smile.

Do your parents allow you and your sister or brother to do that kind of thing at home? I should think not. If you did, someone would be hurt. The reason they aren't hurt on TV is because it is not real. Those people are just actors who are specially trained. You should never try that kind of thing at home, or anywhere else.

When you see people hurting one another, whether it is on TV or real, do you think it is all right? Of course it isn't. The Bible is very clear about how we are to treat one another. It tells us to treat others the way we would want to be treated. Does anyone know what we call that rule? Yes, it is called the Golden Rule.

Would you want someone to call you an ugly name? No! Would you want your friend to hit you? Of course not. Would you want someone to help you if you were hurt? You surely would. If you were sad, would you want a friend to comfort you? I would.

How about at your house? Do you treat your sisters or brothers the way you want to be treated? Do you tease them or take their toys or hit them or make them cry? When you do those kinds of things, you are doing bad things unto them, and they will probably do them back, if they get a chance.

By doing good things for one another, we are not only a help, but we are also doing what God called us to do. And that is to do good and loving things to one another. The next time you are tempted to do something rotten to someone else, ask yourself, "Would I want to be treated that way?"

PRAYER: We know the Golden Rule, Lord, but we do not always follow it. Help us to remember your great love for us when your Son, Jesus, died to take away our sins. Remembering that love, help us to do loving things to one another. Amen.

PRAISE GOD!

OBJECT: Handbell

THEME: We should praise God in song, music, and prayer.

SCRIPTURE: Shout for joy to the Lord, all the earth.
Worship the Lord with gladness;
come before him with joyful songs.
—Psalm 100:1-2

LESSON: This morning there is something in the box that you have seen lately in our worship. It is a handbell. Listen to the sound this bell makes. (*Ring bell.*) Isn't that a pretty sound? This one bell sounds nice, but when all the bells are played together, it sounds even better.

This set of handbells was given to our church. Recently, when two older members of our congregation died, their family decided to give the church a gift that could be used to praise God. And because of their generous gift, we now have a new way to make beautiful music in our worship.

It is very easy to play this one handbell. It is more difficult for all the bells to be rung in such a way that a whole song is played. But when our handbell choir practices and plays together, the sound is beautiful.

Earlier, I said that handbell music is a way of praising God. To praise God means to honor God. Can you think of other ways we honor God in our worship services? Yes, when Young Believers or the choir sings, that is honoring God. What else? Right. When we all sing a hymn, we are praising God. We also honor or praise God when we pray, or when we think about how much we love God. Even putting money in the offering plate is honoring God. Now that you know what praising God is all about, maybe you will feel more like being a part of worship.

PRAYER: We thank you, O God, for the wonderful gift of these handbells. We are glad that they can be used to praise you. Help these young children to be a part of our praise and worship. Let them know that you love them. Amen.

FRESH EVERY MORNING

OBJECT: A small loaf of bread or a piece of bread

THEME: We learn to trust God.

SCRIPTURE: "No one is to keep any of it until morning."
However, some of them paid no attention to Moses; they kept part of it until morning, but it was full of maggots and began to smell.—Exodus 16:19, 20

LESSON: My lunch is in the box today. Look at this little loaf of bread. The only problem is that someone forgot the lunch meat, lettuce, tomato, and mayonnaise. It won't be much of a sandwich with just the bread. Oh, you say it wasn't meant to be my lunch?

How many of you like bread? About half of you. How can you ever eat a sandwich, if you don't like bread? I see. You don't eat sandwiches.

In some countries, bread is the main part of many meals. Jesus talks about bread several times. Bread was also very important when Moses led the Hebrews out of Egypt.

God provided white flakes called manna, which fell on the ground. Every day, the people would gather it to eat. But they were to gather only what they needed for that day, no more. Some people gathered more, just in case God did not provide manna the next day. But whenever they did that, the extra manna would spoil.

God had a good reason for telling them to collect only enough for one day. He wanted the people to learn to trust him every day, rather than to trust their own ability to gather a large amount. It would have been easy for them to forget how important God was, even for their daily food.

We can make the same mistake when we trust ourselves instead of God. Some people don't say a prayer of thanksgiving before their meals, because they, not God, bought the food at the grocery store. But they need to ask who gave them a job that provides money to buy the food? And who provided sunlight and rain so the food could grow? God is the One who provides even our daily bread. We need to trust God.

When we try to do things all by ourselves, many times we mess it up. But if we trust God to help us, he will lead us in the right way.

PRAYER: We are glad we are strong, O Lord. But we are glad that we can trust in you. We tend to make many mistakes, but you lead us to the right things. Amen.

LOOKING GOOD

OBJECT: Hand mirror

THEME: It is not God's way to judge people by the way they look.

SCRIPTURE: But the Lord said to Samuel, "Do not consider his appearance or his height, for I have rejected him. The Lord does not look at the things man looks at. Man looks at the outward appearance, but the Lord looks at the heart."—I Samuel 16:7

LESSON: See how pretty I look. This mirror makes me look like the prettiest person in church. Why are you laughing? I thought you would agree with me about how good looking I am. But obviously you don't agree.

Many of us judge people by the way they look. Many times we dislike people just because they look different from the way we look. Maybe we even pick our friends by the way they look. That is not a smart thing to do. You cannot tell what people are like by the way they look.

When the prophet Samuel was looking among the sons of Jesse for a new king, he liked the appearance of one son. God told Samuel not to consider the boy's good looks, because God had rejected him. He was rejected because of what God saw on the inside, in his heart. That son was not the leader or the lover of God that God wanted.

God had chosen David, who was still a boy. He was not big or strong. He didn't look like a king, but God had chosen him because David loved God. God called him "a man after my own heart."

A person may look good on the outside but be mean and nasty on the inside. God can see that. And he can see what each of us is like on the inside. We can't keep secrets from God.

PRAYER: We can pretend that we are good people, O Lord, but you know what we are really like. Help us to be even better on the inside than we look on the outside. Amen.

BEING A CHRISTIAN IS BOTH EASY AND HARD

OBJECT: Coin

THEME: We should love God more than anyone or anything.

SCRIPTURE: "Good teacher," he asked, "what must I do to inherit eternal life?"—Mark 10:17*b*

LESSON: Thank you for bringing this money to me. This is my pay for having the Junior Sermon today. Oh, you expect this coin back? Now I am poor again.

How many of you collect money? No one here collects money? How many of you have a piggy bank or have some money in a big bank? Oh, now all of you answer yes. Well then, you all collect money. If you are saving it in a bank or in a piggy bank or in savings bonds, you are collecting money.

Some people think money is bad. I don't. If you think money is bad, you can bring all your money to me, and I will take that bad stuff away from you. The Bible doesn't say that money is bad. The Bible says that it is wrong to love money.

Some people love money so much that there isn't enough room in their lives to love other people. And worse yet, they don't have room to love God. That is the problem with the man in our scripture today.

He was a good man, and he wanted to follow Jesus. He wanted to know what he had to do to inherit eternal life, to live forever. Everything Jesus told him to do, the man said he had already done. But when Jesus told him to give his money away, the man was sad and walked away. He loved his money more than he loved Jesus.

How many of you would like to lose all your money? No one. How many of you would like to lose your love for Jesus? Again nobody. If you had to choose between Jesus and your money, the decision might be much harder.

We should always love God first. Money should never be first. It is hard, sometimes, to put God first and allow money to be way behind.

PRAYER: Lord, we thank you for money, but help us not to love it. Help us to love you and one another first. Amen.

A SQUIRT GUN FOR CHURCH

OBJECT: Squirt gun

THEME: There are proper times to use what God has given us.

SCRIPTURE: There is a time for everything, and a season for every activity under heaven.—Ecclesiastes 3:1

LESSON: All right! There is a squirt gun in the box today. I like squirt guns! How many of you own squirt guns? A squirt gun is a fun thing to own. You just fill it up with water and blast someone.

The gun I am holding has one problem. It doesn't have any water in it. How can I have fun if I don't have any water to squirt? How can I have fun squirting your parents with an empty gun? You think that is funny? Do you think your parents would think it is funny if I squirt them in church? You don't think so?

You are probably right. I don't think your parents would like to be squirted with water in church. Most of them would think that church is not the proper place to play with squirt guns. Not because squirt guns are bad, but because we come to church to worship God, not to squirt water.

There is a time and place for squirt guns. The time is when you are playing with your friends, and the place is outdoors. Squirt guns seem out of place in church or school or on the new carpet at home.

Right now is the time for worship. We read the Bible, pray, sing, and talk about God. We can do all these things at other times, but this is the one time and place for doing all of them together.

The Bible says that there are proper times for everything. There is a time for worship and a time for play. A time to work and a time to laugh. A time to go to school and a time for vacation. They are all right in their proper times. God has planned it that way.

I'll give your squirt gun back. I know you will not fill it up until after church. When you are playing with your friends, squirt them once for me. And have fun.

PRAYER: Thank you for our fun and play times, Lord. We enjoy things like squirt guns. We thank you also for this special time of worship. Amen.

TROUBLE CAN BE STOPPED

OBJECT: Squirt gun

THEME: By forgiving, we can stop arguments.

SCRIPTURE: Do not repay anyone evil for evil. . . . Be kind and compassionate to one another, forgiving each other, just as in Christ God forgave you.—Romans 12:17; Ephesians 4:32

LESSON: Squirt guns can be a lot of fun. I have always enjoyed squirt guns on a hot summer day. It feels good to get wet when you are so hot.

We have had a few squirt-gun battles around our house on hot summer days. We start out with squirt guns, but before long we are using buckets and the garden hose. Our battles always end up with everyone completely wet. No one seems to mind that we get carried away with what started as a simple squirt-gun battle.

I can imagine that at your homes too, little things lead to bigger things. Your brother bumps into you in the hall, so you push him back. Then he punches you in the arm. So you hit him in the stomach. Before you know it, both of you are in trouble with your parents, all because of a bump in the hall.

Do you know how to stop a bump from ending up in a fight? The best way is not to get started. If your sister or brother pushes you, your natural response is to push back. Do you know of any place in the Bible where Jesus says that when someone pushes you, you are to push back as hard as you can? Jesus never said anything like that.

Jesus said that we are not to fight back with our fists. We fight back by forgiving and loving other people. Our job as Christians is not to win a fight. Our job is to share with others the love of God through Jesus. We can't do that if we are beating them up.

We are even to love people who say bad things about us. Remember, Jesus asked God to forgive those who crucified him, because they didn't really know who they were killing. He showed us how to truly love others.

Now you and I must follow his example by forgiving and loving others. By following the example of Jesus, we can stop arguments or fights even before they begin.

PRAYER: Dear God, we thank you for showing us the way to stop arguments and fights. Help us to forgive others when they hurt us. Help us also to love others, with the love of your Son, Jesus. Amen.

PLANTING TIME

OBJECT: Packet of seeds

THEME: There can be no harvest if we fail to plant God's Word.

SCRIPTURE: Whoever sows sparingly will also reap sparingly, and whoever sows generously will also reap generously.

—II Corinthians 9:6

LESSON: Look at the pretty flowers in the box today. Aren't they beautiful? What do you mean, there are no flowers in the box? Of course there are. I'm holding them right here in my hand, and the packet says that these are Marigolds. But I have noticed that they do not smell like flowers. They smell like paper. (*By this time, the children will be exclaiming that the packet contains only seeds, not flowers.*)

Let me get this straight. You are telling me that the reason my flowers don't smell is because they are not flowers. And you say that my flowers are not flowers because they are only seeds. Did I say that correctly? So what I have here are seeds, not flowers.

So if I plant one of these seeds, I should have lots of flowers, just like the picture on the package, right? No, I'll only have a few flowers? Well, I must need to plant two seeds to have a lot of flowers. Are you kidding me? I need to plant many seeds to have lots of flowers?

That reminds me of our scripture lesson today. Paul reminds us that serving God is a lot like planting a garden. If we want to see many flowers, we must plant many seeds. If we want to see many of our friends believing in Jesus, we must tell many friends about Jesus. Neither friends believing in Jesus nor flowers happen on their own. You and I must plant the flower seeds, and for others to believe, we must plant God's Word by telling them of Jesus.

I know many people who would like their families and friends to come to church with them. Do you think those family members and friends will come all by themselves? I don't, either. Do you think they might come if we invite them to come with us? They probably would. Most people who come to church for the first time come because a friend or family member invited them.

You and I need to tell others about Jesus, so that with God's help, our friends and family will believe in him. I'm going to plant these seeds, so that I can see many Marigolds bloom. Will you help me talk about Jesus, so that we can see many people believing in him? Great!

PRAYER: Dear God, help us to be able to talk with our friends and family about Jesus. We want to see a great harvest of believers come to you. Amen.

ONE BIG FAMILY

OBJECT: A puzzle piece

THEME: Everyone is needed to make up the family of God.

SCRIPTURE: Just as each of us has one body with many members . . . so in Christ we who are many form one body, and each member belongs to all the others.—Romans 12:4, 5

LESSON: I know where this puzzle piece belongs! This must be the missing piece from a puzzle we have at our house. In fact, it could be the missing piece from several puzzles we have.

Did you ever put a puzzle together and find that you are missing one piece? I see that several of you have. That is something that makes me very upset. All that work to put together hundreds of pieces, only to find that the picture is incomplete.

I feel as though I am wasting my time putting together a puzzle with a missing piece. I never would have started the puzzle if I had known about that piece. I could have found better things to do with my time. Without all the pieces, the puzzle isn't complete.

The church is a lot like a puzzle. All the people in the church are like the individual pieces of a puzzle. The big pieces and the small pieces make up the whole picture, just as big people and little people make up the whole church. Each person depends upon all the other people to make a whole church.

But just like a puzzle, we are not whole if everyone is not working together. If people stay home from church, or skip Sunday school and Bible study, or don't help with the work in the church, we are like a puzzle with some pieces missing. We are not complete.

When Paul wrote the letter to the Romans, he called the church a body. He said that there are many parts to a body, but all the parts work together. What if your elbow didn't want to work with your shoulder? What would you do if your right foot wanted to go to the movies, while your left foot wanted to stay home? All the parts of your body need to work together.

And the church is like that. There are many of us in the church, just as there are many pieces to a puzzle or parts to a person's body. And when all of us work together, we are a whole, complete church for God. All of us are needed to make things work. The church needs young people and old people, married people and single people, men and women, girls and boys—all working together to do God's work.

Each one of you is important. If you are missing, we would be like a puzzle with a piece missing. You are always wanted and needed in the church.

PRAYER: I thank you, dear Lord, for everyone in this church. Help us all to know how important we are to make this church whole. Amen.

THE PRICE HAS BEEN PAID

OBJECT: Postage stamp

THEME: The cross is our sign that Jesus paid the price for our sins.

SCRIPTURE: For the message of the cross is foolishness to those who are perishing, but to us who are being saved it is the power of God. . . . You are not your own; you were bought at a price.
—I Corinthians 1:18; 6:19c-20a

LESSON: We have a postage stamp in the box today. This is an old stamp. It is much older than any of you. No, it is not older than I am.

We all know that stamps are used on letters that we send and receive. The stamp on a letter tells the postal worker that the postage for the letter has been paid. Do you know what happens to a letter that doesn't have a stamp on it? Well, if it has your return address on it, it will come back to you for postage. If your return address is not on the envelope, the letter goes to the dead-letter office, because the price of the stamp has not been paid.

Our scripture today says that a price has been paid for us. Jesus died on the cross to pay the price for our sins. Because of his cross, we have forgiveness from our sins.

A stamp is the sign that a letter has been paid for. The cross is the sign that we have been paid for. We use the cross everywhere to remind us that Jesus paid the price for us.

Have any of you seen a cross lately? (*Take answers.*) Yes, there is a cross on the communion table. And there is one on the wall behind the choir. Look, she has a cross on a chain around her neck. There are also crosses at both entrances to the sanctuary, on our hymnbooks, on the lights, and on the Christian flag.

We do have many reminders that we have been paid for. But of all the crosses I have ever seen, there are two that are the most precious to me. One was made by my son, and one was made by Katie. Both of them were made from pieces of scrap wood. What makes them precious is the love that went into making them—the same kind of love that Jesus had for us.

The next time you see a postage stamp or a cross, remember that it was Jesus who paid a price for us to be free of sin.

PRAYER: Thank you, God, for reminding us every day of the price Jesus paid. Help us to be proud of the cross. Help us to always remember that it is your love that has given us the cross. Amen.

PLAIN AND SIMPLE

OBJECT: Small box of breakfast flakes

THEME: God isn't interested in how fancy we are.

SCRIPTURE: On the outside you appear to people as righteous but on the inside you are full of hypocrisy and wickedness.

—Matthew 23:28

LESSON: Look at this box of breakfast flakes. How many of you would choose these flakes as your favorite cereal? No one would choose these? Let me guess. You probably would choose Munchy Crunchy Sugar Flakes or Toasted Marshmallow Fruit Blobs.

And I imagine that you like the breakfast cereals that have toys in the box. Have you seen the one that has a live gorilla inside? I like the one that contains a toy airplane that can carry three kids and a dog ten miles. You know I am joking!

It seems, though, that we want to buy breakfast cereal because it is the crunchiest and sweetest, with the best toys in the box. No one seems to care whether it is good for you, and that is the real purpose of eating cereal. Instead, we are more concerned about the fancy box, the name, or what kind of toy is in it.

Sometimes we do the very same thing in the church. We worry more about how fancy our clothes are than about serving God in a plain, simple way. We don't realize that God isn't concerned with how fancy we are. But God is concerned that we do right things. We should worship God every day, not just on Sunday in order to make people think we are good.

PRAYER: Lord, we need your help to do good things. We don't want people to think we just appear to be religious. We want them to know that we belong to you. Amen.

TEMPTED TO QUIT

OBJECT: First-place ribbon

THEME: Being a follower of Jesus takes a lifetime.

SCRIPTURE: "I have fought the good fight, I have finished the race, I have kept the faith."—II Timothy 4:7

LESSON: Somebody has won first place. This blue ribbon is the sign of first place. Red ribbons usually mean second place, and white ribbons usually mean third place. Blue is the color that everyone wants to win.

When I was a teenager, I entered many displays in the county fair. I won many blue ribbons, several red ribbons, and a few white ribbons. Do you know the difference between winning a blue ribbon and a white ribbon? Yes, to win a blue ribbon, your display or project must be better than the others. The reason it is better is usually because more work has gone into it. Hard work can be the key to doing anything better.

In the scripture lesson, Paul tells us that he has done his very best. In his ministry, he has worked hard, and now he has come to the end of his life and he has been faithful to God. God didn't give Paul a blue ribbon, although he could have. Paul never quit.

Have you ever wanted to quit? When you were having a tough time in school or at home, have you ever wanted to give up? I have, and I think you probably have too. Sometimes we find it very hard to be a Christian. Maybe someone makes fun of us because we go to church or say grace at lunchtime. It would be easy to pretend that we are not Christians and just quit.

Paul knew that being a Christian was like running a very long race. We work at being Christians every day of our lives. The long race is not over until we go home to be with God.

Many people believe that being a Christian should be easy. All we should have to do is believe in Jesus, and then the rest of our lives should be perfect. But Christians get sick, and we have to take tests, and we make mistakes, and we have problems. We can be tempted to quit. But Paul encourages us by telling us that he has remained true to God. And we know that we can do the same, even when we are tempted to quit.

PRAYER: Dear God, please help us when there are rough times in our lives. Help us to know that you are always with us and that we can finish the race, just as Paul did. Amen.

SPRINGTIME

OBJECT: A flower, or a child's drawing of a flower

THEME: We should be excited about knowing Jesus.

SCRIPTURE: They took palm branches and went out to meet him, shouting, "Hosanna!"

"Blessed is he who comes in the name of the Lord!"

"Blessed is the King of Israel!"—John 12:13

LESSON: Look at this pretty flower that was drawn for us. This flower reminds me of spring. How many of you have flowers starting to poke their heads through the soil in your yard? In our yard, we have snowbells and crocus blooming, with daffodils coming up quickly. Spring is a time of blooming flowers.

When I think of flowers and springtime, I also think of Easter and Palm Sunday. Flowers remind me of celebrating, and Easter and Palm Sunday are special days for celebrating.

Do you remember the story we retell on Palm Sunday? From your answers, I can see that each of you has at least part of the story in your mind. Let's go over it again to make sure we all know what happened.

As Jesus came into Jerusalem that day, there were many people on the road. As he rode the donkey over a hill called the Mount of Olives, he would have seen Jerusalem. His disciples and other people were waving palm branches and placing them on the road.

They were also calling out the words from our scripture lesson: "Hosanna!" "Blessed is he who comes in the name of the Lord!" and "Blessed is the King of Israel!" They were calling Jesus the Son of God. Maybe they all weren't aware of what they were saying, but they certainly were excited.

Have you ever been excited? You have? When? This morning when the children's choir came into worship singing and waving palm branches? I was excited too. Most of the time, we sit in church very nicely and quietly. This morning it was fun to get excited and a little noisy.

You know, I think it is just fine with God if we become excited and noisy about Jesus. When the Jewish leaders told Jesus that he should make his disciples be quiet, Jesus told them that if the disciples didn't make noise, then the rocks along the road would. He was saying that it is OK to be excited and noisy.

This picture of a flower doesn't make much noise. But it does remind us that God wants us to be excited about Jesus.

PRAYER: Lord, I thank you for Palm Sunday and for all the people who were excited in Jerusalem that day. I also thank you that we can be excited today. Thank you for Jesus. Amen.

WHICH WAY DO I GO?

OBJECT: Compass

THEME: Jesus points the way to God.

SCRIPTURE: "I am the way and the truth and the life. No one comes to the Father except through me."—John 14:6

LESSON: I know what this is. It is a compass. Do any of you know what a compass is used for? Yes, it can help you to find directions.

I want all of you to point toward the north. I am glad you guys are not leading me into the woods. We would be lost before we even got started. That is when a compass would come in handy.

This little needle on the compass always points toward the north. If you know you need to go east, you head in the right direction by lining up these arrows. (*Show the children how a compass works.*)

When I go hiking, I always take a map and a compass with me. Together, they keep me from getting lost. They point the way for me. Can you think of anything else that points the way? Yes, road signs do that. They tell you the route numbers and tell you when a curve is coming. Your parents or teachers can also point the way for you, by telling you what is good and bad.

In our Christian lives, the Bible can be like a map to help us see how we should behave. And the Bible tells us that Jesus points the way to God. Jesus tells us that he is the only way to get to God.

If I wanted to travel to the hospital (*pick a nearby landmark*), I could choose to go one of several ways. I could cross the Hickory Street bridge, or the Glade bridge, or the by-pass bridge. If I were lost, a compass and a map might even help me get there another way.

But there is only one way to get to God, and that is to believe in Jesus. We can't reach God by being good people, or by going to Sunday school and church every week. And we can't reach God by worshiping a tree or a rock. The only way to reach God is by believing that Jesus is God's Son and that he forgives our sins.

Many people can tell you about God, but only the Son of God can lead you to God. Trust that Jesus is the only way.

PRAYER: I am glad that on Earth, Lord, you have given us many things to keep us from getting lost. Thank you for the Bible, which tells us about Jesus. And thank you for Jesus, who leads us to you. Amen.

GROWING FRUIT

OBJECT: Potting soil

THEME: Like a tree planted in good soil, God wants us to bear fruit.

SCRIPTURE: And we pray this in order that you may live a life worthy of the Lord and may please him in every way: bearing fruit in every good work, growing in the knowledge of God.

—Colossians 1:10

LESSON: This is very interesting, Chris. This looks like a small bag of potting soil. Am I right? I am. I've never received anything like this in the box before.

How many of you plan to go home and eat potting soil for lunch? None of you. I don't blame you. I don't believe potting soil is good for anything at all. Should we just throw it out? What did you say, Chris? Potting soil is good for growing plants, but not for eating? You are correct. Many flower and vegetable plants start growing in potting soil.

Although I would never eat it, if we use potting soil correctly, it can help us grow good things to eat. I use potting soil to start vegetable plants in my house for spring planting. I know that if I take care of the plants, the potting soil will help me raise tomatoes, peppers, and other good things to eat.

God wants us to follow his Son, Jesus, so that we, too, will grow like plants and produce good things (fruit) with our lives. We don't plant vegetables just to look at. We plant them so that they will give us good things. God called us to follow Jesus so that we can do good things for him.

Can you think of any good things we can do? Yes, we can bring groceries into the food pantry to help others have enough to eat. We can help people with their work. We can say nice things to people so they will feel better.

If we plant something in potting soil, it can produce good fruit. And if we follow Jesus and his teachings, we can do good things for God.

PRAYER: We thank you, God, for helping us to grow plants that produce good things. Help us to produce good things for you. Amen.

JOYFUL NOISE

OBJECT: Student book for piano

THEME: Give the best you have to God.

SCRIPTURE: The trumpeters and singers joined in unison, as with one voice, to give praise and thanks to the Lord.

—II Chronicles 5:13a

LESSON: Is this your piano book? You must be learning how to play the piano. Do you think you are doing well? Great!

I happen to know that several of you are learning to play musical instruments. And some of you are taking singing lessons, but you aren't aware of it. If you are in the children's choir, you are taking singing lessons. So almost all of you are taking music lessons of some kind.

Music, I believe, is very important. I love most kinds of music. And the main reason is that when I was your age, I started taking trumpet lessons and joined the elementary band. When I went to junior high, I played the baritone horn. In ninth grade, I joined my church choir. And later on, I taught myself to play the guitar. Learning to play an instrument can be the beginning of a lifelong love of music.

Music is an important part of our worship, too, isn't it? We have organ music, piano music, handbell music, adult choir, Young Believers, congregational singing, soloists, and much, much more. Without music, the worship service would seem dull. Music can be a very important part of worship.

We find in the Bible many times when the people were called to sing, shout, and dance before God. In those days, music, although much different from our music today, was an important part of worship. Do you think God wants us to praise him with music? It would seem so.

I hope that music becomes an important part of your life. And I hope you use your music to praise God.

PRAYER: Thank you, Lord, for music. We enjoy the many different sounds. We are so glad that we can make music that is pleasing to you, though we don't always like to practice or take lessons. Help us to work hard to make beautiful music for you. Amen.

PRACTICE MAKES PERFECT

OBJECT: Student book for piano

THEME: To get better, we need to practice.

SCRIPTURE: I have seen a son of Jesse of Bethlehem who knows how to play the harp.—I Samuel 16:18a

LESSON: I have a feeling you must be taking piano lessons when I see this student book. Am I correct? I thought so. Do you like to play the piano? Good!

How many of you are learning to play an instrument? Wow! I didn't know so many of you were taking lessons. I think it is good for you to be learning to play an instrument. You will never be sorry about what you are doing.

I remember taking trumpet lessons in third grade. Because I took lessons, I know the part you like best about learning to play. I'll bet you all like to practice. Oh my, such moans and groans! It almost sounds as if you don't like to practice. In fact, I'm sure you don't!

Do you think you will become very good on your instrument if you never practice? Of course not. But you would much rather play with your friends or watch TV than spend time practicing. I know which is more fun, but we need to look at which is more important.

The benefit of learning to play an instrument will be with you for the rest of your life. You won't ever remember the playtime you missed to practice. On the other hand, you won't remember all of your playtime, either. And when you are grown, your music will be more important to you.

I know of another young person who probably didn't like to practice, but it was plain to see that he did practice. His name was David. He would become King David. He was such a good harp player that someone who heard how good he was hired him to play for King Saul. He had to practice to become that good.

If you practice, you may get a chance to play for important people. Or maybe you will just enjoy playing for yourself. Either way, you will never get better if you do not practice. So keep practicing.

PRAYER: Lord, most of us don't like to practice. We would rather do fun things. Help us to be faithful in learning to play an instrument, even if it means practicing. Amen.

WE DON'T DANCE IN CHURCH!

OBJECT: Dance shoes

THEME: There are many ways to praise God.

SCRIPTURE: Let them praise his name with dancing
and make music to him with tambourine and
harp.—Psalm 149:3

LESSON: Are these dance shoes yours? They are? Do you take dance lessons? You take tap and ballet? Very good.

How many of you take dance lessons? I see a few hands, but they all belong to girls. Do any of you boys take dance lessons? No? It is OK for boys to take dance lessons too. When I was in junior high, my older sister taught me how to dance. If it hadn't been for her, I still wouldn't know how to dance.

Did you know that the Bible talks about dancing? Well, it does. Some of you might think that the Bible says that we shouldn't dance. Let me read our scripture for today and show you what God says about dancing.

The Bible talks about dancing as a way to praise God. In the past we have talked about praising God with music and singing. And now today, God shows us how we can also praise him with dancing.

Just last week at the Library Theatre, there was a ballet performed by Christians to praise God. It was one of the most meaningful worship services I have ever experienced. As the dancers floated across the stage, it was easy to see that they were praising God. I wish you could have been there.

Maybe some of you girls and boys will practice hard and dance to praise God. It is not just singing or playing music that praises God. You can also dance to praise God. I would love to see you dance and praise God. Whenever you are ready, let me know, and I will be there to worship God with you.

PRAYER: Lord, I am glad you have given us so many ways to praise you. I thank you for these young arms, legs, and voices that were made to praise you. Bless them. Amen.

HAPPY BIRTHDAY!

OBJECT: Birthday card or candles

THEME: Each of us is special and loved.

SCRIPTURE: Look at the birds of the air; they do not sow or reap or store away in barns, and yet your heavenly Father feeds them. Are you not much more valuable than they?—Matthew 6:26

LESSON: (*sing*) Happy birthday to me. Happy birthday to me. Happy birthday, dear Doug. Happy birthday to me.

You seem to think it is funny for me to sing "Happy Birthday" to myself. Don't you sing "Happy Birthday" to yourself? No? I guess I always do, because I like birthdays so much. I don't like just my own birthday; I like all birthdays! Just think of all that cake and ice cream! Don't you just love birthdays?

Today really isn't my birthday. I just started singing to myself because of these candles in the box. Does anyone have a birthday this week? Great! Are you going to be twenty-three? No, just eight.

Why is your birthday different from mine? I know we were born on different days, but don't we all celebrate Thanksgiving, Easter, Christmas, and the Fourth of July at the same time? Well then, why don't we celebrate all our birthdays on the same day? No answers?

Well, I am glad we don't celebrate all our birthdays on the same day. Each of our birthdays is our own special day, and it helps us to feel special.

And God wants us to know that we are special. In Matthew, we are told that God makes sure the birds are fed, even though they do not plant crops and harvest them. God loves them very much. Then Matthew reminds us that to God, you and I are even more valuable than the birds.

As I look at each one of you today, I am reminded of how valuable you are to God. God made each of you special. Whenever your birthdays come, I hope the candles on your cakes remind you that God loves you and made each of you a very special person.

PRAYER: Thank you, dear Lord, for these special children. I am so glad that you love them. Help them to know how special and loved they are. And help us parents and friends to teach them to love you. Amen.

I HAVE MAIL!

OBJECT: Letter or postcard

THEME: Many books in the Bible were letters.

SCRIPTURE: "To Philemon our dear friend and fellow worker."
—Philemon 1*b*

LESSON: Someone gave me a letter. I love to get mail. Do you like to receive mail? Sure, we all like to get mail. Your parents may not like some of the bills that come in the mail, but most of the mail you receive is fun.

This letter isn't really for me. Let's pretend that this letter is for me, though. And let's pretend that this letter is from someone who loves me very much and wants me to know more about God. If all that were true, I would tell you about the things in this letter. I might even read the letter to you. I also might let you copy the letter so that you could read it over to yourself. That way, my letter would help you to know more about God also, and to feel loved.

Some of the books in the New Testament were letters written to churches and to people. Those churches and people read the letters out loud, and even allowed others to copy them. That way, a letter written to the church in Corinth might end up being read in another city. What the writer wrote to Corinth might also be of help to someone else in another town.

Our scripture today is part of a letter written by Paul to a man named Philemon. It is a very personal letter about a slave who belonged to Philemon. Even though my name is not Philemon, there are many good things in this letter for me to learn. I am so glad that Philemon shared this letter with other people, so that all of us can learn what God wants to teach us.

We all like to receive mail. Many of the books in the Bible are God's letters to all of us. We need to read our mail.

PRAYER: Thank you for Philemon and the others who shared their letters, Lord. We are glad we can learn from the Bible. Amen.

BE MY VALENTINE

OBJECT: Red-paper heart

THEME: How do we love one another?

SCRIPTURE: This is the message you heard from the beginning: We should love one another.—I John 3:11

LESSON: What a pretty red heart! Is this my valentine from you? It is! You make me feel good. This is such a nice valentine. Thank you.

Most of you probably are getting ready for Valentine's Day. You go out and buy the valentines, write the name of each person in your class on an envelope, and take them to school. Don't forget to sign them, so your classmates will know who gave them those valentines.

Sometimes we are embarrassed about sending valentines, because we think Valentine's Day is a time to show people we love them in a way that leads to kisses and hugs. It can be that, but it doesn't have to be. Let me tell you of one old tradition about Valentine's Day.

This tradition is about a man named Valentine, who was a priest in Rome many, many years ago. He was put in jail for helping Christians get away from the soldiers who wanted to kill them. While he was in jail, it is said that he cured the jailkeeper's daughter of blindness and taught her about Jesus. She was kind to him while he was in jail, and the night before he was to be killed, Valentine wrote her a note to thank her for her kind acts. He signed it, "Your Valentine."

So you see, Valentine's Day started with a priest and a young girl who loved Jesus. And because they loved Jesus, they loved each other.

It is easy to love people who love us and do nice things for us. It is much harder to love people who are not nice or who may not love us. Do you think it would be hard to love someone who is in jail? Well, maybe it would be easy to love Saint Valentine, because he was a nice man. But could you love someone who had robbed a store or hurt someone and had been put in jail? It would be hard.

The youth group of our church is packing valentine boxes for the prisoners of our county jail. This is the second year it has done this. It is not being done because the people in jail are good, but because they need to know that someone loves them. Our young people, just like the jailer's daughter, are trying to say, "Because we know the love of Jesus, we are trying to share that love with you."

Can you think of someone who might need to hear that they are loved? Maybe it is someone at school, or a neighbor, or maybe even someone in your family. If you love Jesus, he can help you show love to those people. Maybe, through your love, they also will learn to love Jesus.

PRAYER: Lord, help us to know that love is more than hugs and kisses. Help us to love the people whom the rest of the world doesn't love. Thank you for Jesus' love for all of us. Amen.

I NEED HELP!

OBJECT: Medical kit

THEME: God is always ready to help us.

SCRIPTURE: God is our refuge and strength, an ever-present help in trouble.—Psalm 46:1

LESSON: Look at all the medical things in the box. I know you have seen things like these at the doctor's office. You might even have several of these items in your home. Let's look at some of them.

This is called a stethoscope. It is used to listen to your heart or lungs. I know you have seen one of these before. Maybe the doctor has put this round end of the stethoscope on your back or chest and has asked you to breathe deeply. The doctor was listening to your lungs.

Here are some adhesive bandages and a thermometer. Your mom or dad has probably used a bandage like this on a scratched knee or a cut finger. And maybe when you have not felt very well, they took your temperature with a thermometer like this.

How many of you have ever been sick? Each of us probably has been sick at some time. With a little help from our parents or a doctor, we usually get well quickly. It is good to have their help.

The writer of Psalm 46 tells us that God is our help in times of trouble. We can't go to God the way we go to a doctor. We go to God by praying.

When you have a test to study for, God can help you concentrate and learn. If you are lost, God can help you stay calm. And God can help you ask for forgiveness when you have done something wrong. Have you ever been afraid or alone? Well, God can be there for you when you pray for help. And when you have a problem you can't talk over with anyone, God will listen. God is always ready to help us. God is a help in trouble.

PRAYER: We thank you for doctors, Lord. When we are sick, they can help us. We thank you for helping us at all times, even when we are sick. Remind us to call for your help every day. Amen.

WHAT DO YOU WANT TO BE?

OBJECT: Building blocks

THEME: We should do all our work for the Lord.

SCRIPTURE: I urge you to live a life worthy of the calling you have received.—Ephesians 4:1

LESSON: What do you think of this? This is a nice scene made with building blocks. Here is a palm tree, a fort, a couple of pirates, and even a parrot. This is very nice. If Matt wanted to, he could move some of these blocks around and make a different scene. That is part of the fun of building blocks. You can do almost anything with them. But no matter how fancy the scene is, it is still made of individual building blocks.

Have any of you thought about what you might want to be when you grow up? Maybe you want to be a teacher, or an astronaut, or a mechanic, or a truck driver. You can be almost anything you want to be. And you can even change your mind before you grow up, and become something different.

When I was a little boy, I wanted to be a garbage collector. As I grew older, I changed my mind. I decided that I wanted to be a math teacher because I did well in math. But then in college, I changed my mind again. I felt that God wanted me to be a pastor.

It doesn't really matter what kind of work you or I do. What matters is that we do that work as if we were doing it for the Lord. If we are doing all our work for the Lord, there is a much greater chance that we will do a good job.

If you become a schoolteacher and do your work for the Lord, you would teach your class as if Jesus were there. If you become a mechanic, you would do your work as if you were repairing Jesus' car. If you are a student in school, you should study as if you were earning the grade for Jesus.

You can be almost anything you want to be. But always remember to do your work for the Lord.

PRAYER: We thank you, Lord, that we can become almost anything we want to be. Help us to do all our work, now and when we grow up, for you. Amen.

WE HAVE NO LIGHT WITHOUT JESUS

OBJECT: Candle without a wick or one with the wick removed.

THEME: Like candles without wicks, we cannot show the world God's love without Jesus in our lives.

SCRIPTURE: "I am the vine; you are the branches. If a man remains in me and I in him, he will bear much fruit; apart from me you can do nothing."—John 15:5

LESSON: It's my turn for the mystery box! Most of you have had a turn to bring something in, and now it's my turn. When you bring your special items for the mystery box, you never let me throw them against the wall or drop them on the floor. Well, look what I can do with what I brought in. *(Give box a good shake.)* I can drop it on the floor and nothing happens to it. What do you think is in here? No, it's not a ball. It sounds like something hard when I bang it around, doesn't it? Let me show you what I brought—a candle!

Now what can we use a candle for? Yes, a birthday cake. That's a good idea. How many of you have candles on your birthday cakes? They don't put candles on my birthday cake anymore; there are so many candles, they're afraid the house would catch on fire!

Let's think . . . what else are candles used for? Yes, to light up dark areas. When the electricity goes out, we can light candles to help us see. On Christmas Eve in our church, we turn all the lights down low and light candles. We call that a candlelight service.

Let's light this candle and see how much light it makes. How much light do you think it will make, since the sun is shining so brightly? A little? Let's see. Look at that! This candle doesn't want to light. I can't light it. This is embarrassing.

Well, I'll tell you the truth. I knew this candle would not light, because there is no wick in it. It's just wax. We can cut through the wax with this knife and see that there is no wick. A candle needs a wick before it can burn. The wax cannot carry the fire by itself, and if we just lighted a wick, it would not burn for very long. The two must be together in order to work properly.

You know that a regular candle has a wick sticking out at the top, and when it is lit it burns, but it burns very slowly. A candle this size could burn for a long time, if the wind didn't blow on it or you didn't jiggle it around. But this candle won't burn because it doesn't have a wick.

This candle is not able to produce light. It will never shine in the dark. We are just like this candle when we don't have Jesus in our hearts. We cannot shine with God's love. We can show God's love only when we know God through Jesus. When we know Jesus, we become like candles with wicks. We produce light.

PRAYER: Lord, I thank you for each one of these young people. I thank you that, just like a candle, each of them has a potential to burn for you.